RAILROADS of
CALIFORNIA

Brian Solomon

Voyageur Press

Dedication

To Stella

First published in 2009 by MBI Publishing Company and Voyageur Press, an imprint of MBI Publishing Company, 400 First Avenue North, Suite 300, Minneapolis, MN 55401 USA

The information in this book is true and complete to the best of our knowledge. All recommendations are made without any guarantee on the part of the author or Publisher, who also disclaims any liability incurred in connection with the use of this data or specific details.

We recognize, further, that some words, model names, and designations mentioned herein are the property of the trademark holder. We use them for identification purposes only. This is not an official publication.

Voyageur Press titles are also available at discounts in bulk quantity for industrial or sales-promotional use. For details write to Special Sales Manager at MBI Publishing Company, 400 First Avenue North, Suite 300, Minneapolis, MN 55401 USA.

To find out more about our books, visit us online at www.voyageurpress.com.

Library of Congress Cataloging-in-Publication Data

Solomon, Brian, 1966–
  Railroads of California : the complete guide to historic trains and railway sites / Brian Solomon.
    p. cm.
  Includes bibliographical references.
  ISBN 978-0-7603-3333-4 (hb w/ jkt)
  1. Railroads—California—History. 2. Railroad trains—California—History. I. Title.
  HE2771.C2S65 2009
  385.09794—dc22
                    2008039798

Front cover: Sierra Railway No. 28 was bought new from Baldwin in 1922. With its bell ringing and whistle howling, this classic 2-8-0 leads an excursion upgrade toward Jamestown. *Brian Solomon*

Frontispiece: In the last glow of evening, a San Diego–bound *Pacific Surfliner* blitzes the platform at San Clemente Pier on May 31, 2008. *Brian Solomon*

Title pages: Tracks glow in the desert sunset on February 10, 1993. This was the Santa Fe's Needles Subdivision (old Needles District) on the Ash Hill grade near old timetable location Trojan in the Mojave Desert. Today, this route is a key to the BNSF's busy transcontinental traffic. *Brian Solomon*

Back cover: Near San Clemente, the former Santa Fe Surf Line reflects the evening twilight. This line was acquired from Santa Fe by regional agencies in 1994 in preparation for expanded passenger services. Today it is one of the most traveled passenger routes in California. *Brian Solomon*

Editor: Dennis Pernu
Designer: Kazuko Collins

Printed in Singapore

CONTENTS

The former Santa Fe Third District is now one of the busiest lines in California. On June 3, 2008, BNSF DASH 9 No. 750 leads a westward double-stack container train at Fullerton on a pleasantly warm spring evening. *Brian Solomon*

ACKNOWLEDGMENTS

The idea for this book has been stirring for at least 15 years, and I daresay I cannot recall who originally suggested it, but Dennis Pernu at Voyageur Press deserves credit for making the old idea new again and contracting me to finally put it all together. In the years that separated the original concept of this book, much has changed in California. Both Santa Fe and Southern Pacific (SP) have been merged off the map. I still find this difficult to comprehend. Now Union Pacific (UP) runs where SP once did and Santa Fe is spelled BNSF, but both railroads run more

trains on the old lines—well, except for the Modoc, which was partly abandoned. Also, there are far more passenger trains today and in places I did not expect to ride them 15 years ago.

A great many people helped me along the way. In the late 1980s and early 1990s, I lived and worked in California and spent many days perusing maps and photographs while learning about the railroad. In these adventures, I traveled with friends whose railroad knowledge, photographic techniques, and biases helped shape my understanding and appreciation of California, including Scott Bontz, Dave Burton, T. S. Hoover, Brian Jennison, Bob Morris, Vic Neves, Mel Patrick, Bruce Perry, Brian Rutherford, and J. D. Schmid. On more recent trips, Travis Berryman, Phil Brahms, John Gruber, and Dan Munson have traveled with me. At the Southern Pacific's offices, Bob Hoppe, Jack Martin, and Bart Nadeau helped me put a face on the SP and made my photography more productive. Mark Hemphill, Dave Stanley, and Richard Steinheimer offered me encouragement at a time when I was very much new to the West. WinteRail, held every March in Stockton, has proven to be a premier venue for photography and, more importantly, a way to meet people who share an interest in railways.

In 1994, Don Gulbrandsen, then editor of *Pacific RailNews,* agreed to publish articles I'd written on the SP and western railroading, and then pulled me away from California by hiring me to work for Pentrex Publishing in Wisconsin. In my two years there, I came to learn much about publishing, writing, editing, and railroading. Most importantly, I got to know many people connected with the industry.

Special thanks also to Fred Matthews, who lent photographs, provided the sidebar on Jack London Square (see Chapter 6), was generous with suggestions on photo locations and recollections of SP, and provided intelligent discussion of California railway history, directing my efforts on a number of topics. Phil Gosney lent photos and provided an interview. Paul Hammond and Kyle Wyatt at CSRM made introductions, answered numerous questions, and heightened my appreciation of the museum and its collection. Joe Bispo and all the volunteers at Railtown 1897 in Jamestown went out of their way to make me feel welcome, while teaching me about the Sierra Railway and assisting with my photography there. Thanks to everyone at WRM for their hospitality and interest in my project. Denise Tyrrell provided information on Metrolink and aided with my research of that commuter network. Doug Riddell made introductions. Chris Goepel arranged photographic sessions on California Northern. Tom Hargadon provided accommodations and transportation on several occasions, as did Mike Fournier, Darrin Gagliarducci, Matthew Graham, Andy Hulse, and Collette Sweeney. Thanks to everyone at Bloom's Saloon in San Francisco. Paul Byer provided transport to the Orange Empire Railway Museum and comparative discussion on technology.

Thanks to all the photographers who lent images for the project and assisted with captioning. In addition to those already mentioned, these include Howard Ande, Bob Buck, Marshall Beecher, Tom Carver, Don Kendall, Tom Kline, Sayre Kos, Elrond Lawrence, George S. Pitarys, Ted Smith-Peterson, and Justin Tognetti.

My family has always been supportive of my research and photography. My fascination with California railroading stems from a very early age when my father, Richard Jay Solomon, bought me a set of Lionel's Santa Fe F3As. Years later, my father, mother Maureen, brother Seán, and I spent two weeks exploring California, including an all-day adventure on the *Coast Starlight* back when steam-heated heritage equipment with opening Dutch doors was still the rule. My father's vast library was mined on many occasions during the research for this book. He proofread the text and lent images. Special thanks to my cousin Stella Costello for hosting me in Long Beach and joining me on exploration of the Surf Line, Sprinter, San Pedro Red Cars, and Metrolink, and for taking part in a sociological study of Santa Fe 3751.

I've consulted more than 100 sources for this text, and an extensive bibliography is included at the back. I'm partial to old timetables, maps, and other railroad company literature, of which I've listed a few of the more useful items. Among the most helpful and interesting enthusiast sources are John Signor's detailed books on Southern Pacific and Union Pacific routes. These books feature a wealth of detail and classic photos. Virgil Staff's *D-Day on Western Pacific* provides a rare level of insight and information on dieselization, while Jeff S. Asay's *Track and Time* provides fascinating detail on operation and track layout. Asay's book also offers great descriptions of long-lost San Francisco street trackage and curiosities such as WP's tunnel under Potrero Hill, abandoned in 1962. Gerald M. Best's *Snowplow: Clearing Mountain Rails* is an old favorite, and I recommend it to anyone interested in Donner Pass. Anthony Perles's books on the San Francisco Muni tell the story of California's most interesting street railway. *Trains* magazine has regular features on California railroading, and articles by Fred Frailey, David Lustig, and others have kept me up to date over the years. I've made every effort to make this book interesting, accurate, and current; any errors are my own and not those of the people who have helped me along the way.

Caltrain's *Baby Bullet* express trains pass at San Carlos, California, in the evening rush hour. Here, an elevated right-of-way is one of several modern infrastructure improvements on this heavily used passenger-rail corridor. *Brian Solomon*

INTRODUCTION

California, geographically the nation's third-largest state, by coincidence also has the United States' third-largest railway network (by route mileage). Its lines total more than 5,300 miles and extend across virtually every type of terrain, running along Pacific Coast bluffs and beaches, across blazing deserts, through redwood forests, and over myriad mountain passes. Tracks have been built from more than 200 feet below sea level to 7,000 feet above it in the high Sierra. These railways are among the most interesting and famous in the world. Who hasn't heard of Southern Pacific's legendary Donner Pass crossing, the late great Santa Fe, or San Francisco's cable cars?

California railroading means many things to many people. To some, it is the sight of a 12,000-ton freight with locomotives fore and aft, winding its way through golden grass-covered hills in the Tehachapis; to others, it is riding Amtrak's *Coast Starlight* with views of Mt. Shasta, San Francisco Bay, and the wide expanse of the Pacific.

Some may enjoy taking a spin on San Francisco's historic streetcars, while many others revel in the state's glorious railroad past through photographs, timetables, and especially by exploring the state's great railway museums and preserved lines.

Historically, California conceived more than 1,500 railway schemes. Many were built and blended into larger systems, while others remained only the dreams of visionaries. Today, two freight railroads account for most of the state's mileage, but there are 24 freight-hauling railroads in total, a half-dozen passenger operators, five light-rail/streetcar networks, two (heavy) rapid transit systems, and a host of preserved railways, museums, and historic sites.

There was once much more. In the railroad's golden age, California hosted dozens of logging railroads, interurban electric lines (including the famed Pacific Electric, once deemed the most extensive of its type in the world), and common-carrier narrow gauge lines. Over the years,

Recalling a bygone era of California logging railroads, Roaring Camp & Big Trees Railroad's Shay locomotive *Dixiana* crosses a wooden trestle among the sequoias near Felton, California. *Brian Solomon*

San Jose-bound Caltrain with F40PH 906 *Burlingame* pauses at San Carlos station on May 6, 2008. The station is at a lower level, indicating the location of the tracks before recent grade-separation improvements put them well above street level. *Brian Solomon*

Sunset on the Sunset Route. A Union Pacific eastward manifest flies east past the Amtrak depot at Palm Springs. In the desert, high winds blow sand through the air, contributing to colorful sunsets. What isn't apparent in the photograph are wind's abrasive effects— the photographer's legs were exposed to the whirling sand and were sore for days after making this image. *Travis Berryman*

many lines have been abandoned and companies merged out of existence. The famed South Pacific Coast Route from San Jose over the Santa Cruz Mountains is largely just a memory. Likewise, the old Southern Pacific narrow gauge Carson & Colorado that ran on the east side of the Sierra range was abandoned in 1960 (yet traces of the C&C remain or have been preserved). Even the mighty Southern Pacific—the driving force in California transportation for many years and by far the state's most extensive and influential railroad—was merged into history in 1996. Today, Union Pacific and other operators run on former SP lines.

A book of this nominal size cannot hope to be any more than a cursory overview of such an extensive and complex railway network. My goal as author has been to introduce California's railways while placing them in both historical and contemporary context, and to highlight the most interesting and exciting elements of their operations. I've touched upon the building of the railways and the personalities involved with planning, financing, constructing, and operating the lines. I've discussed operations, stations, trains, cars, and locomotives. What makes California's railways special are the places served, so I've tried to show the most intriguing railway venues. Although I've tried to cover many areas and aspects of railroading in the Golden State, I've not attempted to discuss everything. This feat would be impossible in the space permitted. Instead, I've dwelled on places, companies, and sites that I've found to be the most interesting, while giving others nominal mentions and leaving others out altogether.

I want this book to convey the spirit of California and to capture the enthusiasm of its railways that has made it one of the greatest railway places on the planet. My success will be judged by you. Enjoy!

Railroads of California

©2008 Illustrations by Otto M. Vondrak. Not an official map. Not all lines and locations shown.

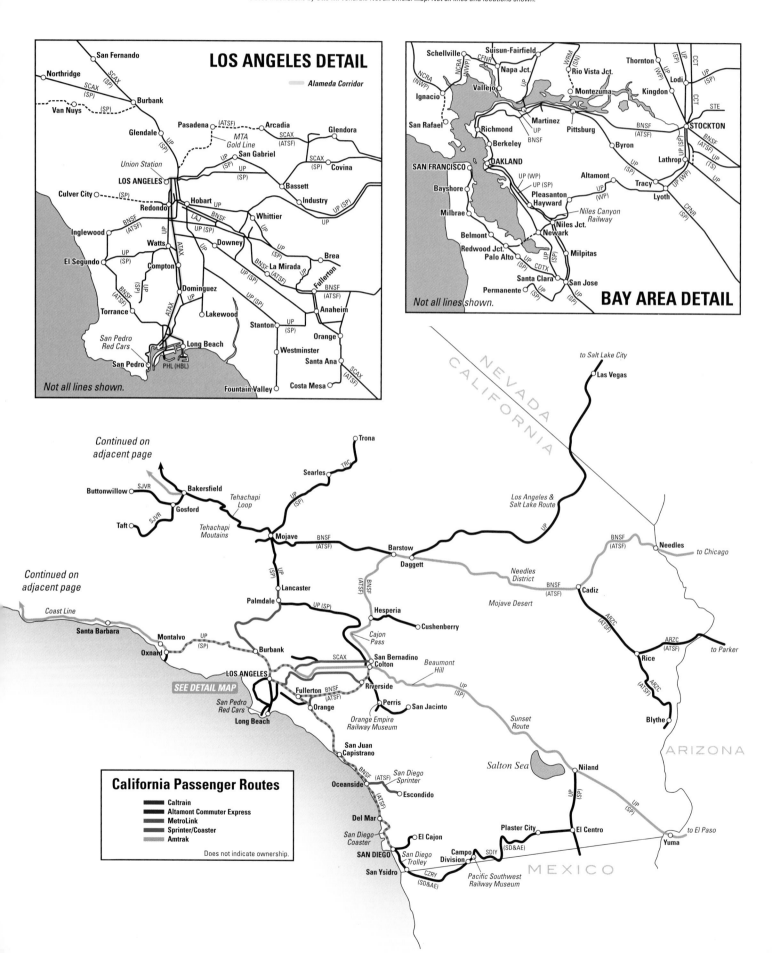

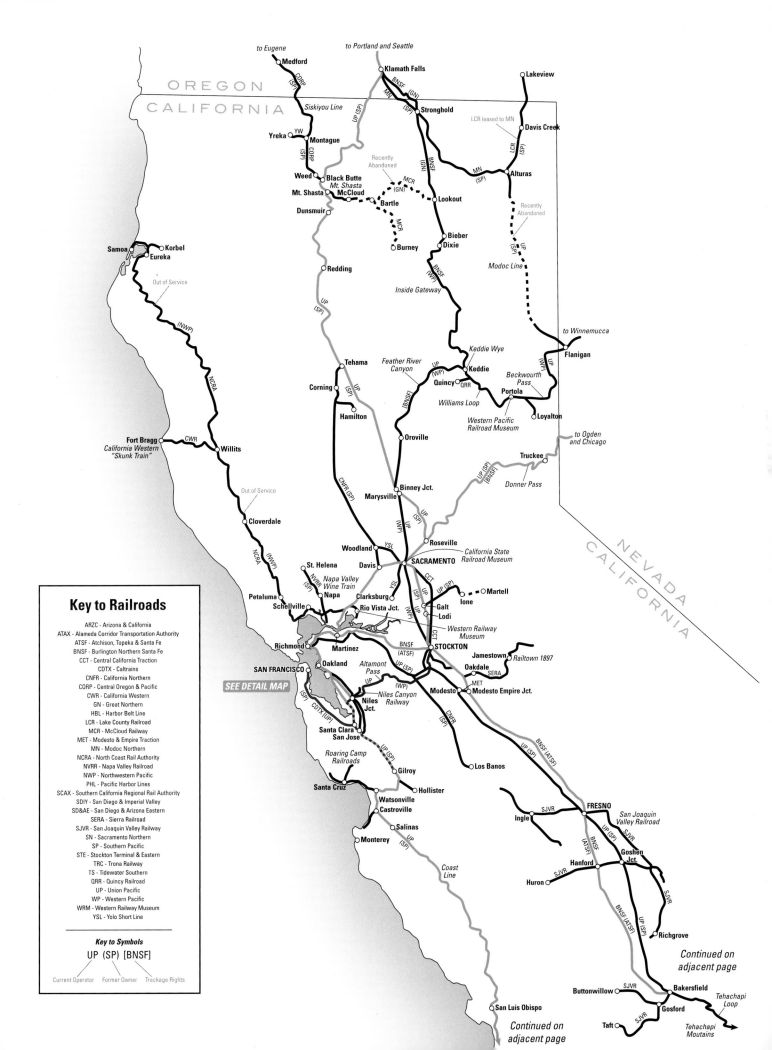

Key to Railroads

ARZC - Arizona & California
ATAX - Alameda Corridor Transportation Authority
ATSF - Atchison, Topeka & Santa Fe
BNSF - Burlington Northern Santa Fe
CCT - Central California Traction
CDTX - Caltrains
CNFR - California Northern
CORP - Central Oregon & Pacific
CWR - California Western
GN - Great Northern
HBL - Harbor Belt Line
LCR - Lake County Railroad
MCR - McCloud Railway
MET - Modesto & Empire Traction
MN - Modoc Northern
NCRA - North Coast Rail Authority
NVRR - Napa Valley Railroad
NWP - Northwestern Pacific
PHL - Pacific Harbor Lines
SCAX - Southern California Regional Rail Authority
SDIY - San Diego & Imperial Valley
SD&AE - San Diego & Arizona Eastern
SERA - Sierra Railroad
SJVR - San Joaquin Valley Railway
SN - Sacramento Northern
SP - Southern Pacific
STE - Stockton Terminal & Eastern
TRC - Trona Railway
TS - Tidewater Southern
QRR - Quincy Railroad
UP - Union Pacific
WP - Western Pacific
WRM - Western Railway Museum
YSL - Yolo Short Line

Key to Symbols

UP (SP) [BNSF]

Current Operator   Former Owner   Trackage Rights

OREGON

CALIFORNIA

to Eugene — Medford

to Portland and Seattle — Klamath Falls

Lakeview

Siskiyou Line

Stronghold

LCR leased to MN

Davis Creek

Yreka

Montague

Weed

Black Butte

Mt. Shasta

McCloud

Recently Abandoned

Bartle

Lookout

Alturas

Dunsmuir

Burney

Bieber

Dixie

Recently Abandoned

Modoc Line

Samoa

Korbel

Eureka

Out of Service

Redding

Inside Gateway

to Winnemucca

Flanigan

Tehama

Feather River Canyon

Keddie Wye

Keddie

Beckwourth Pass

Corning

Quincy

Hamilton

Williams Loop

Portola

Loyalton

Fort Bragg
California Western
"Skunk Train"

Willits

Oroville

Western Pacific Railroad Museum

to Ogden and Chicago

Truckee

Donner Pass

Binney Jct.

Marysville

Out of Service

Cloverdale

Woodland

Roseville

California State Railroad Museum

St. Helena

Davis

SACRAMENTO

Petaluma

Napa Valley Wine Train

Napa

Clarksburg

Rio Vista Jct.

Galt

Lodi

Martell

Ione

Schellville

Western Railway Museum

Richmond

Martinez

STOCKTON

Jamestown

Railtown 1897

SAN FRANCISCO

Oakland

Altamont Pass

Oakdale

Modesto

Modesto Empire Jct.

Niles Jct.

Niles Canyon Railway

Santa Clara

San Jose

Roaring Camp Railroads

Gilroy

Los Banos

Santa Cruz

Hollister

Watsonville

Castroville

Salinas

FRESNO

San Joaquin Valley Railroad

Ingle

Goshen Jct.

Monterey

Hanford

Coast Line

Huron

Richgrove

Continued on adjacent page

Buttonwillow

Bakersfield

Tehachapi Loop

San Luis Obispo

Continued on adjacent page

Gosford

Tehachapi Mountains

Taft

NEVADA

CALIFORNIA

PART I
HISTORY

After the announcement of the discovery of gold near John Sutter's mill in 1848, California—which would gain statehood in 1850—underwent rapid population growth. Though travel to the Golden State was slow, expensive, and dangerous, tens of thousands of settlers, fortune seekers, and opportunists made their way west. Among the more popular paths was the Overland Route, which roughly followed the path of the Platte River Valley across the Nebraska plains, then through the territories of Wyoming and Utah, and across the Nevada desert to the foothills of the Sierra. Difficulties reaching California, combined with the area's growing population and booming economy, led men to seek a faster, safer link to California from the East. A railroad to the Pacific Coast had been under consideration since the 1830s, but financing and engineering obstacles seemed insurmountable.

By the 1850s, railroading was clearly the most attractive method of land transportation. However, reaching California would require nearly 2,000 miles of new construction across difficult and largely unpopulated terrain. Most railroads were still relatively short—often less than 100 miles in length. The longest continuous railroad in the United States operated by one company was the famous broad gauge Erie Railroad. Completed in 1851, the Erie was just over 400 miles long, connecting the lower Hudson Valley to Dunkirk, New York, on Lake Erie.

At the highest elevations, Central Pacific's Donner Pass route was enclosed in show sheds and colloquially known as "railroading in a barn." When the sheds impaired operations by making it difficult to introduce automatic block signaling, the railroad introduced a British-designed electric staff system that authorized train movements using metal staffs issued to the train crew. Electrically interlocked telegraph instruments ensured only one staff could be issued at a time. By employing relatively short block sections, trains could follow fairly closely with an absolute separation between them. At its maximum extent, Donner's electric staff system controlled 98 route miles—probably the most extensive application of such a system on any American railroad. *Munson Paddock collection, Railroad Museum of Pennsylvania, PHMC*

CHAPTER 1

EARLY RAILROAD HISTORY

Financing woes complicated railroad access to California. Most successful railroads had been built with capital raised privately, although a state or municipality would occasionally back the project or offer direct financial support. Access to capital had slowed progress of many lines. Even railroads with expansive visions tended to subsist on local traffic until major end points were reached and greater sources of traffic tapped. How could a company raise money to build across hundreds of miles of plains and desert with no established population and little prospect for traffic? In Washington, D.C., a few farsighted men recognized the need for a railroad that spanned the continent. In 1852, U.S. Secretary of War Charles Magill Conrad was given a congressional mandate to locate the best routes for a Pacific railroad. That year, California chartered its first line, the Sacramento Valley Railroad (SVRR). The iron wheels were in motion.

Facing page: East of Colfax, Central Pacific's climb over Donner is briefly interrupted. The line drops into Long Ravine and begins climbing again around the rocky promenade called Cape Horn, where tracks were cut into a rock shelf hundreds of feet above the river. In this 1878 vintage glass-plate photograph, a locomotive crew poses at Cape Horn, then considered one of the scenic highlights of the line. Today, this is the eastward track; the westward line misses the view, using a pair of tunnels through the rocks. *Munson Paddock collection, Railroad Museum of Pennsylvania, PHMC*

Above: Central Pacific's original Sacramento Depot was the western terminus of the Transcontinental Railroad. Today, the site is occupied by the California State Railroad Museum. *Brian Solomon*

SVRR's chief engineer was a bold, visionary young man named Theodore D. Judah. New England–born, he was among the most talented railway engineers in the United States and had proven his merit on difficult projects before moving west with his wife, Anna. Judah worked fast, completing a 23-mile line between Sacramento and Folsom within a few months. The first public train operated on August 17, 1855, a remarkably early date to operate a railroad in such a distant place as California, isolated from the heavy industrial complexes of the East. Yet Judah's sights were greater than just the SVRR, which would never be more than a dead-end branch. (Today, part of the route is used by Sacramento's light-rail system.)

Judah's passion was to conquer the Sierra: one of the great impediments to linking California with the East. To many people, these mountains were a rock wall—an impenetrable row of snow-crested peaks. Judah was seen by many as a fool as he searched for a passage to carry a railway. But he was not alone in his vision. Undaunted by naysayers, Judah made crossing the Sierra his life quest. In today's world, where many people are rigidly defined by their career parameters, it is difficult to appreciate Judah's exceptional versatility and capabilities. The multitalented polymath personally surveyed known Sierra crossings,

laid out much of the railroad line, drummed up local interest, engaged in politics in Sacramento, San Francisco, and Washington, and enticed the necessary financial support. He lobbied Congress and the president, and is understood to have had a personal hand in drafting the Pacific Railroad Act, which authorized the building of the Transcontinental Railroad.

The act specified that the Pacific Railroad was to link the Missouri River and Sacramento. Why Sacramento? In the 1850s, the state's population was focused in central California. The trip between Sacramento and the San Francisco Bay was made easily by ship, and Sacramento was well established as an inland port. It was there in 1861 that Judah convinced four established Sacramento business owners—Charles Crocker, Mark Hopkins, Collis P. Huntington, and Leland Stanford—to finance his railroad. These men came to be known as "the Big Four." Conveniently, that same year, Leland Stanford won election as governor of California.

The urgency of the railroad was felt in Washington as a result of Civil War politics. A transcontinental line was seen as key to linking California with the Union rather than the Confederacy. With Judah's urging, President Abraham Lincoln signed the Pacific Railroad Act in July 1862, legislating federal land grants and cash to the railroads that would build the line. To speed construction, the act established two railroads to build toward one another. From the west, the Central Pacific (CP) followed Judah's survey over the Sierra and east across Nevada and Utah; from the east, the Union Pacific was chartered to build toward CP from the Missouri River. Generous grants accompanied each mile of line completed. The race was on, with each railroad hoping to cash in on as many miles of grants as possible.

On January 8, 1863, Central Pacific initiated construction in Sacramento with a lively public ceremony—commemorated by a pictorial mural inside Southern Pacific's (now Amtrak's) Sacramento passenger station—with Leland Stanford

Sacramento was the original western terminus of the first Transcontinental Railroad. A large mural in the 1926-built Southern Pacific station depicts the famous groundbreaking ceremony held in 1863. *Brian Solomon*

An 1868 glass-plate view of Central Pacific's Truckee yards, shortly after the line over Donner Pass opened. *Munson Paddock collection, Railroad Museum of Pennsylvania, PHMC*

turning the first shovelful of earth. The groundbreaking was merely symbolic; 10 months passed before the first rails were laid.

Judah, the visionary, never lived to see his railroad completed. He was a purist and an idealist. Nineteenth-century business practices had little regard for his high-minded attitudes, and the Big Four rapidly quelled his involvement. With hopes of raising funds in the East for a buyout of the Big Four, Judah traveled via ship and overland at Panama, where he contracted an incurable tropical fever. He died in New York in November 1863 at age 37.

Despite federal incentives, Central Pacific made slow progress in its early years as it pecked away at the Sierra

crossing. By 1865, it had only built into the foothills near Auburn, just 35 miles east of Sacramento. The Civil War, a major cause of insufficient labor in California, was among the impediments to CP's progress. Charles Crocker addressed the lack of able-bodied men by looking to China. To finish the line, he ultimately employed an estimated 14,000 Chinese laborers who pushed CP to the spine of the Sierra at Donner Summit in July 1867. When the Donner Pass crossing in California was open in May 1868, tracks were already being built across the Nevada and Utah deserts.

On May 10, 1869, CP and UP met in the legendary, stage-managed, "golden spike" ceremony at Promontory,

This posed view of an eastward train on the Long Ravine trestle dates from about 1868–1869. Between 1876 and 1942, the Nevada Country Narrow Gauge passed below the bridge to make a connection with the main line at Colfax. The wooden trestle was replaced years ago, and today's double-track line runs on twin parallel steel tower-supported plate-girder viaducts, while four lanes of Interstate 80 run through the valley below the railroad. *W. A. Lucus collection, Railroad Museum of Pennsylvania, PHMC*

Utah. Having turned the first earth, the Big Four's ever-keen politician, Leland Stanford, contributed in the hammering of this "final" spike. A telegraph wire attached to the spike transmitted a simple signal telling the world that America's coasts were united by a common railway—sort of. It was a great publicity stunt. Photographs were exposed of locomotives facing one another, and long-winded speeches were followed by rivers of champagne. While regular freight and passenger service commenced over the new tracks a few days later, and travel to California was cut from weeks to days, the real railroad-building had just begun.

Big Four Dominate California

The joining of transcontinental rails represented just one step in the Big Four's development of a comprehensive transportation system for California. Although often portrayed as having been motivated by greed, the Big

Four's reasons for dominating California transport were much more complex. While Promontory connected dots on the map, the railroad was far from finished. The transcontinental line was so crudely built that much work was needed before it could handle substantial traffic. Equally important was construction of links to the Bay Area and feeder lines.

Traffic didn't develop immediately. In fact, traffic was very light in the early years. Many people (including the Big Four) feared the Transcontinental Railroad might prove a white elephant. The Big Four faced a choice: they could either divest themselves of the railroad or expand it to secure more traffic. Since they were unable to sell out at a satisfactory price, they continued to build.

Stanford was the frontman, the public face. Crocker was the builder. Hopkins served as the accountant. Huntington, who had the best business sense of the

Central Pacific built wooden snow sheds over much of its line between Blue Cañon and Andover. Deemed necessary in times of heavy snow, the sheds proved to be a liability in drier months. To minimize the risk of fire, CP stationed fire trains at key locations. This one was photographed with 4-4-0 *Grey Eagle* at the old Blue Cañon station, an important operations center and crew change until completion of Donner double-tracking. *W. A. Lucus collection, Railroad Museum of Pennsylvania, PHMC*

quartet, was the brains behind the Big Four. A shrewd judge of character, Huntington was rarely on the losing side of a business deal. He also would be the longest lived of the Big Four, shaping the evolution and dealings of western railroads until his death in 1900.

The Big Four brought a new level of complexity to business. Their trail of leases, holding companies, subsidiaries, and affiliated companies was often deliberately convoluted. Carefully manipulating details of their arrangements, both for business and for political gain, their railroad enterprises grew and prospered faster than any others in the West. Their domination of California business is legendary, as was the perception of a gross abuse of power that left a legacy of distrust and suspicion that lingered for decades after their passing.

The potential for serious competition to the Central Pacific had started before the golden spike was struck.

Competitive schemes emerged both inside and outside of California. The Big Four sought to quell local competition by acquiring or controlling emerging California railroads. By the early 1870s, they had their fingers in just about every significant line proposed or underway in the state.

Bay Area Connections

Although Sacramento was CP's initial western terminus, San Francisco had always been the real goal. A few months after Promontory, the Big Four established a Bay Area connection by way of a CP affiliate called the Western Pacific (not the twentieth-century railroad of the same name) that was built via Tracy and over the Coast Range via Altamont Pass. The WP's route gave CP the vital toehold it needed on the Oakland waterfront opposite San Francisco, while trans-bay ferry operations provided access to the city. The Big Four melded these operations under

San Francisco Belt Railroad Alco S-2 No. 23 rests at the railroad's engine house at Lombard and Embarcadero streets in San Francisco about September 1971. Although not busy after 1970, this waterfront short-line railroad was once vital to San Francisco shipping, operating numerous spurs and branches that served the city's piers. Today, portions of the Belt's former right-of-way host Muni streetcar tracks. The engine house is now an office, and trackage remnants can be seen in pavement leading to the old locomotive stalls. *Fred Matthews*

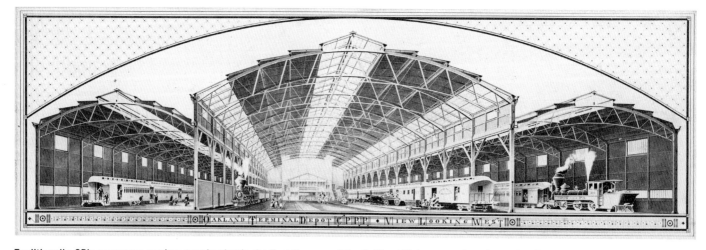

Traditionally, SP's passenger services terminating in the East Bay served the Oakland Mole, a massive pier on San Francisco Bay covered by a cavernous Victorian-era train shed. This period drawing shows SP's Mole in profile. In 1958, SP ended San Francisco–Oakland ferry services, closed the Mole, and began terminating trains at nearby Oakland 16th Street Station. *Railroad Museum of Pennsylvania, PHMC*

the Central Pacific banner. (Three decades later, another scheme would revive the Western Pacific name.)

Another Sacramento–Bay Area route was established by the California Pacific Railroad, a company originally independent of the Big Four. The "Cal-P" was incorporated in 1865 and began construction between Vallejo and Sacramento in 1867, completing the route in 1869 with a lightly built line. The Cal-P served San Francisco via a direct ferry connection from its Vallejo terminal. Although initially designed to augment the Central Pacific, the Cal-P had rapidly emerged as CP's competitor. Soon after the opening of the Transcontinental Railroad, Cal-P's shorter route captured the lion's share of local passenger traffic between San Francisco and Sacramento. Furthering the Big Four's annoyance, Cal-P also had transcontinental visions

of building via the Feather River Route and Beckwourth Pass. In 1871, the Big Four took control of Cal-P, and the Central Pacific formally leased the line in 1876. Under Big Four control, the Cal-P route was developed as a key link from Sacramento to Oakland. A line was extended to the Benicia waterfront, and beginning in 1879, CP established a new route to Oakland using train ferries across the Carquinez Straits to Port Costa. From there, another railroad along the shores of San Pablo Bay reached the Oakland waterfront. This mainline ferry arrangement survived until 1930, when the straits were finally bridged. The old California Pacific has been largely forgotten, and while only a portion of its line is part of the present-day Sacramento–Oakland route, railroaders still refer to this as the "Cal-P."

A pair of former VIA Rail FPA4s lead the Napa Valley Wine Train northward through its namesake valley in its first season of operation in October 1989. This former SP route had a long history. In 1871, Central Pacific inherited the line when it took control of California Pacific. Today, the Wine Train is one of the region's finest dining trains. *Brian Solomon*

CHAPTER 2

SOUTHERN PACIFIC

Another competing transcontinental scheme was formulated in the mid-1860s. The San Francisco & San Jose Rail Road (SF&SJ) connected its namesake cities in June 1864. Within a few months, the principals behind the SF&SJ incorporated the Southern Pacific, a line initially envisioned to connect San Francisco and San Diego by way of Los Angeles and provide a link with a line to be built west from the Missouri River. Congress authorized the Southern Pacific to build east from San Francisco to the Colorado River, where it was to meet the Atlantic & Pacific.

SP's architects envisioned its main line running southeast of San Jose, via Gilroy, then over Pacheco Pass and across the San Joaquin Valley, over the Tehachapis, and across the Mojave Desert to Needles near the Colorado River. In March 1869, SP reached Gilroy, a little more than 30 miles south of San Jose. By that time, however, the Big

Facing page: A glass-plate image from about 1912 finds a pair of dapper gentlemen posing in front of Southern Pacific's new Santa Barbara station that opened in January 1906. SP 2286, a Baldwin 4-6-0, leads second No. 10. At that time, SP train 10 was the *Sunset Express,* operating from San Francisco to L.A. via the Coast Line. In those days, operating authority was provided by timetable and train order rules. These rules enabled more than one section (locomotive and cars) of a given train schedule to run on the same timetable authority. On this day, at least two sections were operating on No. 10's timetable; second No. 10 might be a special train or a section of the *Sunset Express. Bay Area Electric Railroad Association at the Western Railroad Museum Archive*

Above: A neon sign at the California State Railroad Museum recalls the Southern Pacific's *Sunset Limited. Brian Solomon*

Four had already taken control of the line and sealed its fate. Although details of the Big Four's transaction remain nebulous, in 1870 the foursome melded the original Southern Pacific, SF&SJ, and associated properties into a new entity called the Southern Pacific Railroad Company under the control of the Central Pacific. CP and Southern Pacific were financially, personally, and operationally intertwined.

The Big Four opted against pursuing SP's planned Pacheco Pass crossing, instead building from a junction on the CP's Western Pacific line at Lathrop southeast (eastward by the SP timetable) through the San Joaquin Valley. This territory was largely open and uninhabited. SP's arrival resulted in the settlement of many San Joaquin Valley communities. By November 1874, the railroad reached the established community of Bakersfield. From there, it built its circuitous grade over the Tehachapis.

To survey SP's route, the Big Four employed William Hood. The SP engineer earned fame for his clever use of a complete spiral at Walong to maintain a steady gradient in the steep confines of the canyon there. Popularly known today as the "Tehachapi Loop," Hood's grade still serves as a main line. Hood continued to engineer SP's lines for years to come. He was promoted to chief engineer in 1883 and served with SP until the 1920s.

In the 1870s, Southern California was little more than a desert. The area supported nominal agricultural enterprises but had few inhabitants. Los Angeles was a village with just over 5,000 people. In 1876, with a new transcontinental railway near their doorstep, L.A. residents feared they would be bypassed. Although a railroad connected L.A. with San Pedro, the latter was not yet a substantial port. The entire region was just an outpost on the edge of the nation. Seeking a connection to the East, Los Angeles enticed the Big Four to detour SP's route. SP's San Francisco–L.A. main line was finished on September 5, 1876, and included construction of the 6,975-foot-long San Fernando Tunnel.

Wasting no time, SP forces kept pushing eastward. Initially, SP bypassed Needles and instead built toward Yuma, Arizona, to head off the Texas & Pacific (T&P), which was working its way west. Upon reaching Yuma, the Big Four finagled the details of SP's charter and continued east across Arizona and New Mexico, intercepting the T&P at El Paso and ultimately reaching New Orleans in 1883. That same year, SP finally constructed a dead-end branch across the Mojave Desert to Needles to intercept Santa Fe forces building along the Atlantic & Pacific charter.

Northward Expansion

In 1869, the Big Four's California & Oregon had started building compass north (timetable direction east). By 1872, its rails had reached the top of the Sacramento Valley. The Big Four tended to be reactive. Expansion to Oregon stalled when they didn't view competition in the Pacific Northwest as an imminent threat and instead refocused resources elsewhere. Northward expansion resumed in the mid-1880s when they found renewed interest in a direct Oregon main line. They forced a line north to meet the Oregon & California, which was building south from Portland. The resulting route, a tortuous line with numerous summits, was known as the Siskiyou Line after the range of mountains it crossed. Especially difficult were the 3 percent grades over Siskiyou Summit just north of the Oregon–California line.

Ultimately the Big Four took control of the O&C, completing its first Oregon main line in 1887. By that time, California had emerged as a prime destination, and the Big Four could not fend off competition indefinitely. However, their railroads had earned tens of millions of dollars and made them among the richest men in America.

In 1884, the Big Four reorganized their properties into the dominant Southern Pacific Company. The old Central Pacific was leased to the Southern Pacific Company, while CP continued to exist on paper well into the twentieth century. From that time onward, however, it was the Southern Pacific Company that remained in the limelight.

E. H. Harriman

Old C. P. Huntington was the last of the Big Four. When he died in 1900, Southern Pacific Company's California-based empire controlled more than 8,000 railroad miles in the United States and Mexico. The railroad was still growing, and in 1901, SP closed the gap on its Coast Line, making for a second San Francisco–Los Angeles through route, via San Luis Obispo.

Change was in the cards for SP. The West's largest railroad was about to grow in a whole new way. An unlikely candidate for a railroad mogul had entered the scene. Wall Street manipulator Edward H. Harriman had had his eyes on the Central Pacific route when he took control of the

Scene at Caved-in Tunnel no. 10
n Cuesta Grade, near San Luis Obispo, Cal.
1910

Aston
Photo
652

In 1910, Southern Pacific maintenance gangs work to install a shoo-fly at the site of Tunnel 10 on the Coast Line's Cuesta grade. The tunnel caved in, temporarily closing Cuesta until SP built around it. Notice the steam shovel working near the collapsed tunnel portal. *Bay Area Electric Railroad Association at the Western Railroad Museum Archive*

bankrupt Union Pacific in 1897. Harriman awed industry watchers with his rapid transformation of UP's business. Huntington's death proved Harriman's opportunity, and he wasted no time seeking not just the Central Pacific route but the entire Southern Pacific system. Applying skillful business acumen, Harriman took 45 percent control of the SP in 1901, remarking, "We have bought not only a railroad, but an empire."

Harriman rapidly made a detailed assessment of his new property. Using prudent judgment and the suggestions of SP's able general manager, Julius Kruttschnitt, Harriman authorized large sums for massive engineering improvements. He aimed to improve the flow of traffic and lower operating costs by improving grade profiles, straightening curves, and adding line capacity.

Significant improvements included better access to San Francisco via the all-new Bayshore Cutoff, improvement of the Coast Line with the Montalvo Cutoff (involving a line relocation between Burbank and Montalvo by way of Santa Susana Pass), and the beginning of Overland Route double-tracking. Smaller improvements included new and longer passing sidings, introduction of standard steel-bridge designs to replace older lighter spans, and installation of significantly heavier rail on key routes. System-wide, Harriman purchased 540 new locomotives—many built to new standardized designs—and ordered nearly 9,000 new freight cars.

Among Harriman's most visible improvements was pioneering the wide-scale application of automatic block signals. His personal concern for safety resulted in many

A bright Los Angeles morning in about 1960 finds that SP extra 6243, led by A-B-B-B-A F-units, has just arrived at Taylor Yard. SP built these yard facilities in the 1880s and in the twentieth century developed the site as its primary L.A.-area classification yard and locomotive-servicing facility. At its peak, Taylor built an estimated 40 freights daily. Its primacy ended when SP opened the new West Colton Yard in 1973. The change was gradual, as Taylor was last used as a classification yard in 1985, and its locomotive facilities survived a few years longer. Metrolink's commuter train servicing facility was built on a portion of the site. *Bob Morris*

Facing page top: Southern Pacific's *Daylight* races past Union Switch & Signal lower-quadrant semaphores on the Coast Line. SP proudly launched its new streamlined *Daylight* on March 21, 1937. Pullman-built consists provided a daily service between San Francisco and Los Angeles via the Coast Line. Each 12-car train had capacity for 584 revenue passengers. The *Daylight* was a superb service offering a level of class and style that has no parallel in California today. *Bay Area Electric Railroad Association at the Western Railroad Museum Archive*

Facing page bottom: The last surviving railroad steam ferry in the Bay Area is the old Northwestern Pacific *Eureka*, preserved near San Francisco's famed Fisherman's Wharf. Before the construction of the Golden Gate Bridge, NWP-owned steam ferries shuttled railroad passengers from terminals in Marin County to downtown San Francisco. *Brian Solomon*

SP main lines being equipped with state-of-the-art protective Union Switch & Signal lower-quadrant semaphores, some of which survived through the end of SP's independent operations into the 1990s. For many years, SP boasted the most miles of signaled main line in America. Although Harriman died prematurely on September 9, 1909, at the age of 61, his plans influenced SP upgrades for another generation.

Harriman also added a number of routes to SP's California map. In 1903, he acquired a 50 percent interest in the Pacific Electric (see Chapter 5). Pushing east from San Diego in 1906, SP joined forces with the Spreckels Sugar interests constructing the San Diego & Eastern (SD&E) along the Mexican border. The line was completed in 1919 to El Centro, California, by way of the spectacular Carrizo Gorge (the SD&E later became an SP subsidiary, the San Diego & Arizona Eastern). In 1907, SP and the Santa Fe joined forces in the Redwood Empire north of San Francisco, participating equally in the Northwestern Pacific (NWP) that consolidated numerous smaller railroads. NWP completed its through route to Eureka in 1914, and in 1927 SP assumed complete control of the line.

Antitrust Action and New Lines

The federal government viewed the UP–SP combination as anticompetitive. After Harriman's death, the Justice Department spent several years disentangling the railroads in a complex legal battle that was further complicated by a related action to separate SP and CP. During that time, America's imminent involvement in World War I resulted in unprecedented federal involvement in the nation's railroads. In an effort to ease traffic congestion and inefficiencies, Congress effectively nationalized the entire network under the United States Railroad Administration.

In the 1920s, control of its lines was restored to private SP management, and control of CP ultimately was resolved in SP's favor, although the SP was separated from the UP. With legal troubles behind it, SP finally completed Donner Pass double-tracking and began construction of Harriman's long-planned Natron Cutoff to Oregon. The new route deviated from the old Siskiyou Line near the base of Mt. Shasta at Black Butte, California. SP's last significant new line in California was the Alturas Cutoff, which opened in 1929. Also known as the Modoc Line, this addition skirted the northeastern corner of the state, having pieced together re-gauged portions of the old Nevada-California-Oregon narrow gauge, plus new construction that provided a more direct route to Oregon from the east. It was a raw railroad—much of the line was laid out on high desert with a minimum of complicated grading.

Southern Pacific SD40T-2 No. 8322 is silhouetted against Mt. Shasta on the Modoc Line near Stronghold, California, on February 12, 1994. SP's 251-mile-long Modoc Line was a shorter route for Oregon freight traffic assembled in the late 1920s. It was 210 miles shorter than SP lines via Dunsmuir and over Donner Pass. After its merger with the SP, Union Pacific closed the Modoc Line as a through route. A short line called the Modoc Northern has operated the Alturas-Klamath Falls section since 2005. *Brian Solomon*

While many main lines have prospered in recent years, not all have faired well. After its merger with SP, Union Pacific closed SP's Modoc Line as a through route, then abandoned the Alturas-to-Wendel section. Remnants of the line are seen at Madeline, California, on July 14, 2003.
Philip A. Brahms

In November 1964, five Alco PA diesels lead Southern Pacific train No. 101 at Martinez, California. The *City of San Francisco*—jointly operated with the Union Pacific and the Chicago & North Western—was SP's first regularly scheduled diesel-powered passenger train. In the 1930s, service was initially provided with an Electro-Motive Corporation articulated streamliner. This was soon replaced by a longer, heavier, diesel-hauled train that operated in various incarnations until the advent of Amtrak in 1971. *Hank Shermund photo, Phil Gosney collection*

SP in the Diesel Age

Through the end of the twentieth century, SP remained California's most prominent railroad, integral to the state's transportation and growth. Although SP made an effort to provide top-quality streamlined passenger services on many routes, ridership declined rapidly after World War II. Despite passenger losses, SP remained among the most progressive American railroads, and from the 1950s onward it focused on improving its freight business. It installed many miles of Centralized Traffic Control (CTC) on its main lines. After World War II, SP diesel-ized all operations, retiring its last domestic steam in 1957. It built new yards to move greater volumes of tonnage. In conjunction with its massive new West Colton Yard (completed in 1973), SP constructed a new freight cutoff between Palmdale and West Colton by way of Cajon Pass that opened in 1967. This cutoff allowed through freight to avoid traversing Los Angeles.

Looking for ways to more efficiently move freight, SP dabbled with German-built diesel-hydraulic locomotives in the early 1960s only to find that the maintenance-intensive machines were ill-suited to California's tough environment. Beginning in the mid-1960s, SP acquired large numbers of high-horsepower six-motor diesel-electrics to replace its postwar four-motor F-units. SP was an enthusiastic buyer of General Motors' Electro-Motive Division 20-cylinder SD45 model and worked with the builder to refine a Tunnel Motor variation using revised airflow that was better-suited to operate in the Sierra. SP's fleet of modern diesels worked in multiple on the head-end and as helpers on tonnage freights. For more than three decades, the powerful sounds of these machines and their 16-cylinder kin were heard across California, reverberating through canyons, roaring through mountain passes, and racing across the deserts.

In the 1980s, SP and the Santa Fe planned to merge but were denied by the Interstate Commerce Commission. Billionaire Phillip Anschutz, owner of the Denver & Rio Grande Western, picked up where the Santa Fe left off, taking control of SP in 1988 and jointly running the two

Above: Although it was constructed to resemble an old adobe structure, the former SP station at Glendale, California, has walls made of concrete and covered by plaster. Historically, Glendale was a popular station with celebrities traveling to nearby film studios. Today, it's part of an intermodal transportation hub serving Amtrak, Metrolink, and city bus routes. *Brian Solomon*

Left: The Spanish revival–style former SP station at Glendale was designed by Kenneth MacDonald Jr. and Maurice Couchot. It was opened in 1924 and served SP's long-distance trains as a Los Angeles suburban stop. Today, Metrolink and Amtrak's *Pacific Surfliner* stop here, but Amtrak's *Coast Starlight* does not. *Brian Solomon*

Top: Southern Pacific 4-8-4 No. 4449 is seen near Hooker Creek, running toward Redding, California, on August 31, 1991. This magnificent locomotive was restored to service in the 1970s. *Brian Solomon*

Above: A westward Southern Pacific freight is stopped on the Cal-P at Davis on the evening of October 17, 1989, shortly after the Loma Prieta earthquake rocked the Bay Area. The earthquake damaged Oakland's 16th Street Station, destroyed area freeways, and resulted in long-term changes to SP's Oakland-area trackage. Railroad lines and a yard were relocated to make room for a new freeway alignment, while new passenger stations were built at Emeryville and Oakland's Jack London Square. *Brian Solomon*

Southern Pacific SD45 7422 leads an amply powered westward freight on the No. 1 track at Yuba Pass on October 4, 1992. With traffic on the rise, Union Pacific is now considering restoring two-main track operation to this section. *Brian Solomon*

railroads. SP's image prevailed for a few more years, but the railroad's best days were behind it, and by the early 1990s it was the weakest of the big western systems. Following the Burlington Northern–Santa Fe combination of 1995, Union Pacific bought SP on September 11, 1996, consummating Harriman's dream with a merger that had been denied by the federal government some three-quarters of a century earlier.

CHAPTER 3

SANTA FE

In the 15 years following the completion of the first Transcontinental Railroad, the Big Four enjoyed a near-total monopoly on California's land transportation. With both Central and Southern Pacific transcontinental connections to California firmly in their grip, they built, bought, or controlled the vast majority of railway mileage within the state. Yet competition was coming. The first to penetrate the Big Four's empire was the Santa Fe Railroad.

The Atchison, Topeka & Santa Fe—more commonly known as the Santa Fe—was the vision of railroad builder Cyrus Holiday, who as early as the 1850s envisioned linking Kansas with the Pacific Coast and Mexico City. Although the Santa Fe was slow to gain momentum, by 1880 the railroad acquired the charter for the Atlantic & Pacific, enabling it to build westward along the route of the old Santa Fe Trail. As with most railroad schemes, this task was neither straightforward nor simple. The Santa Fe faced numerous political, financial, and geographical challenges as it vied with other schemes in its passage west.

Facing page: Pulling toward Lavic, a westbound BNSF intermodal train crests the grade near Ludlow on the BNSF's former Santa Fe Needles Subdivision. Despite the remoteness of California's Mojave Desert, its easy access, wide-open spaces, and very heavy traffic have made this route popular with photographers during the cooler winter months. *Ted Smith-Peterson*

Above: The Santa Fe emblem is embedded in the side of the former Atchison, Topeka & Santa Fe station at Riverside, California. The Santa Fe and Union Pacific served Riverside in stations located one block apart from one another. Both stations have since been adapted for new uses, while Metrolink's modern Riverside Downtown facility is just a few blocks west of the historic stations. *Brian Solomon*

Under the able leadership of William Barstow Strong (who from 1877 served as the railroad's general manager and vice president, and as its president beginning in 1881), the Santa Fe made remarkable progress. Strong was crucial in shaping the Santa Fe's route structure during its formative period. Arthur M. Johnson and Barry E. Supple, in *Boston Capitalists and Western Railroads*, quoted Strong as saying in 1882 that "in the United States… the power of a Railroad to protect and increase its business depends upon its length, and the extent of the territory it can touch."

The Big Four watched with alarm as the Santa Fe pushed the A&P westward. They hoped to intercept the A&P's entry to California in 1883 by constructing an SP line eastward across the vast, barren expanse of the Mojave Desert from the village of Mojave (at the base of the eastern slope of SP's Tehachapi crossing) to Needles (near the west bank of the Colorado River that divides Arizona and California). This strategy was a nineteenth-century technique oft-used to outfox a competitor. It was a risky maneuver: if the competitor had sufficient capital, it might simply build around the line constructed to block it, leaving a railroad with a long branch and no traffic (or at least insufficient traffic to support two railroads). Initially, the Santa Fe had applied a different strategy: it bypassed California entirely and constructed a through line to the Pacific via Mexico. This move not only threatened to squash the Big Four's visions of Mexican expansion, but also gave the Santa Fe the appearance of being able to divert transcontinental Pacific trade to its Mexican port (although in practice this route never handled a significant volume of Pacific trade). Faced with this quandary, the Big Four backed down, and in 1884 SP sold its route from Needles to A&P as part of an exchange that opened Mexico to expansion by the Big Four.

Simultaneous with its A&P construction, the Santa Fe established connections in Southern California. San Diego desired eastward railroad connections and presented itself as a logical Pacific terminal. In 1880, the California Southern Railroad (CS) was formed by the Santa Fe and interests in San Diego to connect with the A&P transcontinental building west. The California Southern surveyed a route north-northeast from San Diego by way of Del Mar on the coast and continuing inland via the rugged Temecula Canyon to San Bernardino. Wasting no time, CS opened the route from San Diego to a connection with the Southern Pacific at Colton in August 1882.

The SP connection initially gave San Diego its desired transcontinental link, but the California Southern's route was doubly flawed and failed to achieve the Santa Fe's objective. Since CS was forced to rely upon the Big Four's Southern Pacific as its eastward connection, SP blocked construction beyond Colton, preventing CS from reaching San Bernardino (and ultimately the Santa Fe, via a connection with the A&P). The second and perhaps more serious flaw was the CS line via Temecula Canyon. Although it provided the shortest practical route east from San Diego toward the A&P, Temecula Canyon proved seasonally prone to violent flooding. CS finally overcame the SP blockade at Colton and reached San Bernardino by September 1882. But the Temecula Canyon line was wrecked by torrential flooding in early 1884. This destruction altered railroad history: while CS funded extensive rebuilding, the high cost of reconstruction devastated its finances, forcing re-examination of the long-term viability of the route. While examining alternative options for California terminals, the Santa Fe had to assume full financial responsibility for CS to keep it out of the hands of the Big Four. (The Santa Fe continued to operate CS as a subsidiary, eventually fully amalgamating it and other Southern California lines into its transcontinental network.)

The last major link in the Santa Fe's planned transcontinental route involved completion in 1885 of the 81-mile line by way of Cajon Pass from San Bernardino to a junction with the Mojave–Needles line at Waterman, California. This strategic junction was later renamed Barstow to honor Santa Fe President William Barstow Strong and was developed as one of the railroad's most important yards and engine terminals. Today, Barstow's modern sprawling facilities are among the most important in the West.

Cajon Pass presented its own challenges. There, CS constructed an abnormally steep grade over the San Bernardino Mountains (the west slope requires an arduous climb greater than 3 percent—significantly steeper than Central Pacific's Donner Pass crossing). Throughout most of the twentieth century, the Santa Fe operated the Cajon Pass crossing as its First District of its Los Angeles Division (see Chapter 7).

San Diego was the Santa Fe's initial western focus, yet the railroad soon redirected its energy toward Los Angeles. Understanding the Santa Fe's change of strategy requires some context. In 1880, with a population of little more than 11,000, Los Angeles was a far cry from the

At San Clemente Pier on June 1, 2008, Santa Fe 3751 leads the first steam excursion over the Surf Line in decades. The former Santa Fe Fourth District is now one of Amtrak's busiest routes. *Brian Solomon*

great urban conurbation it is today, and San Diego was deemed a superior natural harbor. Yet the inadequacies of the California Southern's original Temecula Canyon line and a greater distance had proven San Diego more difficult to reach. Equally important was the enormous developmental potential of the Los Angeles Basin. Despite an inferior natural harbor, L.A. simply had more to offer. Ultimately, the investments of the Santa Fe and other railways contributed to L.A.'s rapid development as a metropolitan area.

The Santa Fe initially tapped the L.A. area using SP trackage rights, but by 1887, the Santa Fe had assembled its own route from San Bernardino to L.A. by way of Pasadena. This became the Second District of its Los Angeles Division, operated as its premier passenger gateway. Not satisfied with one line, the Santa Fe soon forged a second link from San Bernardino to L.A. by way of Riverside and Fullerton, which opened in 1888. Known as the Third District of the Santa Fe's Los Angeles Division, it traversed Santa Ana Canyon and opened the "Orange Empire" to development. This route was longer than the Second District, but its low-grade profile emerged as the Santa Fe's preferred freight line, and it remains the BNSF's primary freight route today.

In the late 1880s, the Santa Fe connected Fullerton with Oceanside, providing a more direct Los Angeles–San

Diego route and allowing closure of the troubled Temecula Canyon line (although portions continued to serve as stub-end branches). Operated as the Fourth District of the Los Angeles Division, this route hugs the Pacific Coast from just below San Juan Capistrano to near Del Mar and became known as the Surf Line.

An important facet of the Santa Fe's California expansion was the role of oil in locomotive development. With no local source of coal, the Santa Fe had to transport fuel over enormous distances. Since oil was plentiful in Southern California (the state would become the world's leading oil producer in the early twentieth century), the Santa Fe encouraged development of oil-burning steam locomotives. Decades before the advent of commercial diesel-electric locomotives, the Santa Fe adopted oil as the choice locomotive fuel for its western lines. Other railroads followed suit, and soon the Southern Pacific, Union Pacific, and Western Pacific were using oil-burning steam locomotives.

Reaching the West Coast helped define the Santa Fe as a serious transcontinental competitor. But in the 1890s, the railroad's finances faltered. It was bankrupt by 1893, reorganized as the Santa Fe Railway. With this change came a new dynamic president, Edward P. Ripley, who led the line from 1895 to 1919. Ripley was crucial in developing the company into one of the great American railroads during the golden age of steel rail transport. Under Ripley, the Santa Fe completed a number of key links in its route structure. Perhaps even more important, although less understood, were his fundamental improvements to the railroad's main lines. Ripley, like E. H. Harriman, recognized the engineering challenges to overcome to put the railroad in first-class condition. Line relocations and grade separations were implemented, minimizing ruling grades and reducing curvatures.

The Santa Fe had effectively initiated an economic boom in Southern California by competing directly with Southern Pacific. Competition lowered rates and fueled a transportation revolution that promoted commerce, encouraged settlement and land development, and spurred the state's economic engine.

Early in Ripley's administration, the railroad expanded California operations by penetrating the heart of the Big

The Santa Fe's old San Francisco & San Joaquin Valley route remains vital to the BNSF's Bay Area access. At 7:59 p.m. on June 23, 2006, former BN SD40-2 No. 6791 leads the eastward Richmond-to-Riverbank local in Franklin Canyon near Christie. Trackage in the foreground is the Asbury spur used to serve an online shipper located between the Collier and Christie passing sidings. *Justin Tognetti*

Four's empire with an extension northward to San Francisco. Looking to overcome SP's monopoly in the San Joaquin Valley, farmers and businessmen in the region initiated construction of an independent railroad called the San Francisco & San Joaquin Valley Railway (SF&SJV). Largely parallel to routes established by SP, the SF&SJV was aimed at connecting with the Santa Fe to provide competition with SP. By 1898, the SF&SJV connected Stockton, Fresno, and Bakersfield, yet the SF&SJV neither possessed sufficient finances to build over the Tehachapis to reach the Santa Fe transcontinental nor to extend its own route westward to reach San Francisco.

The Santa Fe took control of the SF&SJV in 1898 and thereupon negotiated rights to use SP's Tehachapi crossing. The Santa Fe had considered its own Tehachapi line, but the high cost of building and operating a duplicative route left the plan in the realm of the theoretical.

Following acquisition of the SF&SJV, the Santa Fe completed the route from Stockton to the Bay Area. This expensive line required traversing the marshy Sacramento Delta and grading through the rugged Glen Fraser and Franklin canyons to reach Point Richmond, where the Santa Fe constructed a terminal and ferry facilities. In San Francisco, the Santa Fe built ferry slips, yards, and sidings on filled land in China Basin. The Santa Fe's Bay Area trackage was less extensive than its L.A. network. It acquired a branch from Point Richmond to Oakland, and from 1907 to 1927 was a partner with SP in the Northwestern Pacific.

Santa Fe All the Way

As California grew, the Santa Fe's key transcontinental route swelled with freight and long-distance passenger traffic. The Santa Fe was the only transcontinental line under one company that operated from Chicago to the Pacific Coast. Other routes were joint efforts. From its inception in the 1930s, the Santa Fe's *Super Chief* was among the nation's most famous trains. This exclusive train came into its own in 1937, when the Santa Fe reequipped it with a flashy Budd-built stainless-steel streamlined consist hauled by Electro-Motive E1 diesels. The *Super Chief* introduced the flashy "warbonnet" paint scheme devised by Electro-Motive artist Leland A. Knickerbocker. The distinctive blend of red, yellow, black, and silver was emblematic of the modern Santa Fe and became the most recognized railway paint scheme in North America.

Experience with passenger diesels demonstrated to the Santa Fe the potential of diesel-electric road locomotives. In 1939, Electro-Motive introduced its famous FT diesel, and the Santa Fe was among the lines to test it. Ultimately, the Santa Fe bought the largest fleet of FTs and had the most significant application of the pioneer machine. During World War II, the Santa Fe dieselized its busy, graded, desert lines east of Barstow where a lack of clean water made steam operations difficult and expensive. This successful mainline dieselization set a precedent for the dieselization of all railroads across North America.

As highway travel and jet planes eroded the Santa Fe's passenger traffic, the railroad skillfully transformed its transcontinental into a premier intermodal corridor. The Santa Fe pioneered the use of top-lifting cranes in 1963, which reduced the time it took to load and unload truck bodies from flatcars. During 1967, the Santa Fe took a leap forward by experimenting with dedicated trailer-on-flatcar (TOFC) trains operated at passenger train speeds. In the 1970s, the Santa Fe further augmented its intermodal traffic by developing its route as a land bridge for container traffic originating in the Far East destined for the East Coast or beyond to Europe. A novelty at first, this business grew rapidly as a result of railroad deregulation, which began in the mid-1970s and culminated with the Staggers Act in 1980. Railroad business was made more profitable with the advent of double stacks, which contributed to lower operating costs. Although the Santa Fe initially resisted double-stack land-bridge traffic for fears that marketing the backhaul space would erode its lucrative domestic intermodal trade, ultimately the railroad embraced the technology.

The Santa Fe merged with the Burlington Northern in 1995 to form the company now known by its initials, the BNSF. Today, the Santa Fe's route to California is the premier "transcon" route, characterized by long double stacks carrying Far East imports and faster schedules for domestic intermodal shipments.

An eastward BNSF intermodal train descends the east slope of Ash Hill and approaches the desolate timetable location of Bagdad, California. The former Santa Fe main line has developed into one of the busiest intermodal freight corridors in the United States. Every day, dozens of double stacks and piggybacks make the dash across the Mojave Desert on the BNSF's Needles Subdivision. *Justin Tognetti*

CHAPTER 4

UNION PACIFIC AND WESTERN PACIFIC

Los Angeles & Salt Lake Route

Schemes to connect Salt Lake City and Los Angeles intrigued late-nineteenth-century railroad builders. At the turn of the twentieth century, self-made copper mogul Senator W. A. Clark of Montana moved to build this route. He recognized the advantage of San Pedro as a potentially important international port and was keen to build a transcontinental link to exploit it. In 1901, he consolidated Los Angeles area terminal railroads while chartering a new company called the San Pedro, Los Angeles & Salt Lake Railroad (SPLA&SL). Initially, Clark envisioned competing with Harriman, who was then assembling his Union Pacific–Southern Pacific empire. Not to be outdone at his own game, Harriman looked to construct his own railroad along the same line. After a few tense months while competing survey and construction crews vied for territory, Clark and Harriman came to a truce. It was obvious there was neither sufficient potential traffic nor space at key passes for two railroads. Clark sold half of his share in the SPLA&SL to Harriman in 1902, which firmly put the railroad in the Union Pacific camp.

Facing page: At 2:43 p.m. on April 10, 1979, a trio of ubiquitous Union Pacific SD40-2s leads extra-east second LABN with 53 cars across the 1903-built Santa Ana River Bridge west of Streeter, California. Union Pacific's Los Angeles & Salt Lake route was its only direct access to California until it purchased Western Pacific in 1982. *J. D. Schmid*

Above: The Western Pacific's Feather River Route herald. *Brian Solomon*

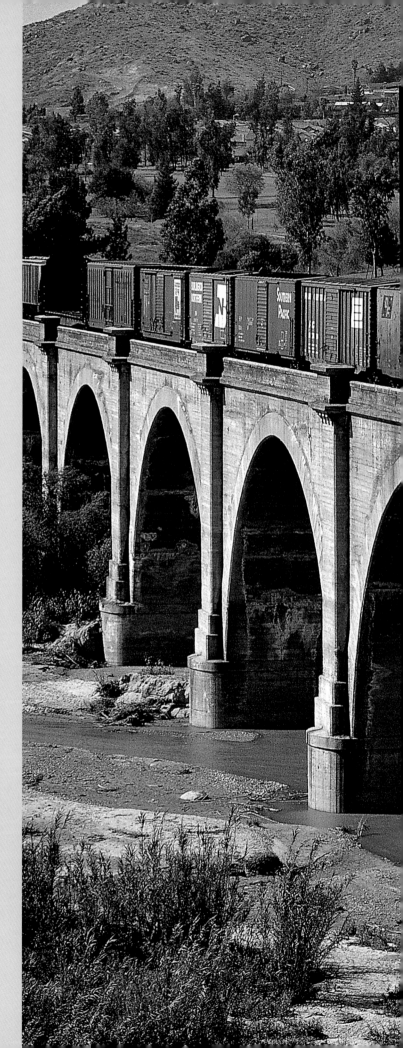

The SPLA&SL was constructed along a southwesterly route across Utah and Nevada from Salt Lake City to Las Vegas. This route negotiated wild, windswept deserts and narrow confines of rocky canyons before reaching the open deserts of Southern California. West of Las Vegas, the line was built over Cima Hill, a rigorous railroad grade that forces heavy trains to a crawl yet seems barely perceptible to the passing observer. Beyond, the line passes through the moon-like environs of Afton Canyon. While the SPLA&SL considered its own route over the San Bernardino Mountains to reach the L.A. Basin, it ultimately opted for trackage rights on the Santa Fe's line from Daggett to Barstow and over the Santa Fe's Cajon Pass crossing to a junction west of Riverside, California. In the L.A. Basin, the SPLA&SL built and operated its own lines.

Railroad-building progressed from both ends of the line, which was completed in early 1905. Within a few months, Union Pacific was offering through passenger and freight services from Chicago to Los Angeles. Among the route's most notable features in Southern California is the massive concrete viaduct west of Riverside over the Santa Ana River. Reinforced concrete was considered a state-of-the-art material when the bridge was completed in 1903, and at the time the span was heralded as the world's largest concrete bridge—an honor it would soon cede to even more massive structures erected by the Delaware, Lackawanna & Western in the East.

After two decades, Clark finally sold his remaining share in the SPLA&SL to Union Pacific, and in the 1920s, UP invested heavily in the route, upgrading tracks and facilities. "San Pedro" was dropped from the name, and the route was generally known as the Los Angeles & Salt Lake. After the federal government forcibly separated Union Pacific and Southern Pacific in 1914, the LA&SL was Union Pacific's only presence in California. It remained that way until UP acquired Western Pacific in 1982.

The LA&SL was known to the public for its great passenger trains, including the famous *Challenger* and *City of Los Angeles* streamliners. Although the traditional era of passenger service ended with the creation of Amtrak in 1971, Amtrak restored long-distance service over the line for a number of years with a *California Zephyr* connection called the *Desert Wind*. This service was cancelled as result of Amtrak's budgetary shortfall in 1997. Far more important than the passenger trains has been the freight traffic that sustained the route since its completion. In the mid-1980s, Union Pacific developed the LA&SL route as one of the first double-stack routes for land-bridge traffic. Traffic patterns have changed since Union Pacific merged with Southern Pacific in 1996, but the route still plays an important role in the UP network.

The Route of the Feather River Canyon

The Western Pacific Railway (WP) was a twentieth-century creation financed by George Gould through his Denver & Rio Grande Western (D&RGW) representing the last American transcontinental railway route. (Gould's Western Pacific should not be confused with the Central Pacific subsidiary that, in the 1860s, constructed track over a portion of the same territory between Sacramento and Oakland. Although the two carried the same name, and in places the lines of the two railroads were parallel, more than three decades of railroad history separate the two companies.)

George Gould, son of the legendary nineteenth-century railroad mogul Jay Gould,

Western Pacific GP20s Nos. 2007 and 2008 lead two F-units with freight tonnage over California's Altamont Pass in 1960. *Bob Morris* ambitiously hoped to create a single coast-to-coast all-rail transcontinental system. This vision had been similarly executed in Canada with completion of the Canadian Pacific Railway, but remained elusive in the United States. The Western Pacific was needed to connect Gould's Denver & Rio Grande Western with the Pacific and circumvent Harriman's recently cemented monopoly of the Salt Lake City gateway.

The WP was organized in San Francisco in 1903. Construction officially began at Oakland in 1906 (although some work in the Sierra was underway in 1905) and progressed simultaneously from several points. In California, WP followed an indirect S-shaped path from the Bay Area to the Nevada state line. From Oakland, the line dropped southeast to Niles Canyon and climbed over Altamont Pass to the San Joaquin Valley. The line ran north–south from Stockton to Oroville via Sacramento, and then via both the North and Middle forks of the Feather River Canyon toward the low saddle of the Sierra at Beckwourth Pass (the name is derived from the explorer who discovered the pass; locally, spelling of his name has been interpreted as "Beckwith," much to the confusion of some observers). The railroad continued east across Nevada by way of Winnemucca and via Silver Zone Pass to Utah, connecting with the D&RGW at Salt Lake City.

The most interesting part—and by far the most difficult to build—was the line through Feather River Canyon. Especially rugged was the stretch east of Oroville along the North Fork of the river. This route had been considered several times for a railroad, but the canyon remained as wild and remote as any place in California. The March 12, 1910, issue of *The Railway and Engineering Review* reported that when WP surveyed the line there was "no means of transportation in the canyon—not even a pack trail." The deep vertical cliffs, loose rock, and great length of the canyon made access and construction challenging. To allow crews to work from multiple points within the confines of the canyon, WP first constructed a wagon road. As built, WP's railroad required 28 tunnels between Oroville and Keddie. Keddie was the limit of WP's original North Fork Division, which constituted a full crew district at the time of completion. East of Keddie, the railroad had fewer bores but required the longest tunnels on the line. WP's longest tunnel—7,306 feet—was at Spring Garden, and its summit tunnel at Beckwourth Pass was 6,006 feet long.

WP was not the first railroad over this low crossing of the Sierra. The Sierra Valley Railway, a branch of the

Nevada-California-Oregon, used this pass at a higher level than WP. Also of interest, before WP's summit tunnel was bored, the railroad crossed by way of a temporary line featuring 3 percent grades. Evidence of these crossings still scars the sagebrush-covered desert above the summit tunnel.

Western Pacific, although significantly longer than Central Pacific's transcon route, has the noteworthy advantage of its low-grade profile. Maximum gradient is just 1 percent, as compared with 2.4 percent on the CP route, and its low crossing of the Sierra, mostly below the snow line, avoids the heavy, wet snow that plagues operations on Donner Pass. To maintain a steady 1 percent climb east of Quincy Junction, the railroad negotiates a full spiral called the Williams Loop, similar to the more famous Southern Pacific spiral in the Tehachapis.

Looking like an N scale model train, an eastward Union Pacific double-stack freight crawls upgrade out of a short tunnel between Poe and Pulga in the Feather River Canyon. Pull-offs along Highway 70 west of Pulga provide views such as this one looking down into the North Fork of the canyon. *Brian Solomon*

WP's completion occurred nearly six months after the fortieth anniversary of the golden spike ceremony at Promontory. It represented a final phase of transcontinental railroad-building, but WP's final spike carried none of the pomp and circumstance of the great Central Pacific–Union Pacific connection. On November 1, 1909, WP track foreman Leonardo D. Tomasso hammered the final connection in place on the now-famous Spanish Fork Bridge at Keddie. Only a handful of people were on site; the railroad's own officers didn't bother to make the trip to see their railroad completed. Most the region's newspapers didn't even mention the event, and it took the trade press several months to mark the occasion.

The railroad town of Keddie is named for the route's surveyor, Scotsman Arthur Walter Keddie, who had long promoted the Feather River Route. While earlier schemes for a Feather River Route floundered, WP's line prevailed, and Keddie, unlike Central Pacific's unfortunate visionary Theodore D. Judah, lived to see his dream completed. As built, Western Pacific had 377 miles of main line in California. Its original charter did not make provisions for branches, so the railroad was a straightforward affair in its original incarnation.

As planned, Western Pacific furnished Gould a key link for his through route from Pittsburgh to the Pacific, but the route suffered from inadequate traffic. Initially, through freight service was provided by just a single train in each direction. WP passenger service began in August 1910 with a pair of long-distance trains; this service was later augmented by local stopping trains on more populated portions of the route. However, much of the WP route across Nevada and Utah is along thinly populated desert expanses. High construction costs and insufficient traffic resulted in insolvency within a few years. On the eve of American involvement in World War I, the Western Pacific Railway was sold at auction, ending its financial ties to the D&RGW. In 1916, it was reorganized as the Western Pacific Railroad.

The new company benefited from traffic growth precipitated by the war and freedom from the constraints of its original charter. WP began to buy and construct feeders to draw more freight traffic to its route. In 1917, WP acquired control of the Tidewater Southern, which served agricultural areas south of Stockton. Then, following financial settlement with the United States Railroad Administration for its role in World War I effort (the USRA essentially nationalized U.S. railroads during the war years), WP acquired the interurban empire of the Sacramento Northern and, a few years later, the old Oakland, Antioch & Eastern electric system, which WP blended with the Sacramento Northern.

The WP's last major line expansion, representing one of the final routes built in the classic railroad era, was construction of its line northward from Keddie to reach a connection with the Great Northern at Bieber Station. This route, known as the Inside Gateway, was completed in November 1931, and it joins the WP's east–west main line on the Spanish Fork viaduct—the famous Keddie Wye. This picturesque double viaduct has long been a favorite location for photographers. Unlike the steady 1 percent of the main line, the Inside Gateway has grades in excess of 2 percent. Never a regular passenger route, this line provided the WP with valuable freight connections and developed into a north–south route in conjunction with the Great Northern and the Santa Fe.

Like most American railroads, the WP dieselized after World War II. It used a variety of builders for yard service, but initially it relied exclusively on Electro-Motive Division's four-motor types for road service. Its fleet of GPs and F-units was augmented in the 1960s and 1970s with a sampling of General Electric diesels. The WP refrained from acquiring high-horsepower six-motor types favored by Southern Pacific.

These truss bridges west of Tobin are among the easily photographed infrastructure in the Feather River Canyon. Highway 70 closely follows the tracks along the North Fork of the Feather River from Poe to Keddie. *Railroad Museum of Pennsylvania, PHMC*

In 1949, Western Pacific, with D&RGW and Burlington, inaugurated one of America's most famous Budd Domeliners, the *California Zephyr*, connecting Chicago and the Bay Area by way of Denver. Originally, it served the SP's Oakland Mole where passengers to San Francisco were conveyed by SP ferries. The daylight run through the Feather River Canyon made for one of the

Detail of the builder's plate on Western Pacific GP7 No. 707 displayed at the Western Pacific Railroad Museum at Portola, California. This 1,500-horsepower GP7 was built by General Motors' Electro-Motive Division in 1952. Under its hood is a 16-567B diesel, the same engine used in EMD's successful F7 and other models of the period. *Brian Solomon*

most scenic journeys in the Golden State. It was the last of the great WP passenger trains. Sadly, in 1970—a year before Amtrak—the much-loved *California Zephyr* Domeliner got the axe, and ever since the Feather River has been a freight-only route (although excursions and Amtrak detours have provided rare opportunities to sample the line). Today, the Stockton-to-Niles section of the line hosts the Altamont Commuter Express suburban trains (see Chapter 10).

Construction of the Oroville Dam on the Feather River North Fork in the early 1960s resulted in a substantial line relocation on WP's route. Approximately 27 miles of the original route were closed, much of it flooded by Lake Oroville. Its replacement was completed in 1962, running compass west of the old line via sidings at Kramm, Elsey, and James (where there is a sharp loop to gain elevation). This heavily engineered line required two very long tunnels (Tunnel No. 8 is the longest on the WP at 8,856 feet), as well as the massive parabolic concrete arch known as the North Fork Viaduct (located deep in the canyon at Intake, the junction of the old and new alignments west of Poe siding).

In the early 1960s, both Southern Pacific and the Santa Fe attempted to acquire WP without success. In 1982, Western Pacific was absorbed by Union Pacific and its main line has been busy with UP's freights ever since.

On June 22, 1984, at 8:40 a.m., Union Pacific's massive DDA40X 6905 leads eastward symbol freight OME at the Rock Creek Bridge in the Feather River Canyon. Western Pacific's Feather River Route was relatively lightly used until UP acquired the line in 1982. Another DDA40X, No. 6946, is displayed at the Western Pacific Railroad Museum in Portola. *George W. Kowanski*

CHAPTER 5

PACIFIC ELECTRIC

America's most extensive and comprehensive interurban electric railway was born in Southern California in the days when Los Angeles and its environs were a paradise of lush orange groves and clean sandy beaches, when the automobile was still a rich man's toy and the skies were clear and unpolluted. With the death of Collis P. Huntington in 1900, his nephew and heir to the Huntington fortune, Henry E. Huntington, was outmaneuvered by E. H. Harriman for control of the Big Four empire. The younger Huntington, however, had ample means, and with an eye for business and railway experience set out to create his own Los Angeles–based railway empire. In 1901, he established the Pacific Electric (PE), acquired control of existing electric lines (including the pioneering Los Angeles & Pasadena formed in 1895), and over the next decade extended lines across the Los Angeles Basin.

Henry Huntington had greater interests than just connecting dots on the map or annoying the Harriman empire, however; his railway development was closely linked to the real estate schemes of his Pacific Electric Land Company. Although it was created as a reaction to, and as a competitor of, Southern

Facing page: Pacific Electric owl-eye car 418 is one of the famous "Blimps" that worked as late as 1961 in L.A.–Long Beach service. It is one of more than a dozen vintage PE cars preserved at the Orange Empire Railway Museum. *Brian Solomon*

Above: Friday through Sunday, the Port of Los Angeles operates replica Pacific Electric Red Cars over a portion of the Pacific Harbor Line's freight trackage. Here, cars 500 and 501 pass near historic San Pedro. *Brian Solomon*

Pacific, the PE proved too successful and too valuable to remain outside the SP empire for long. SP bought into PE in 1903, and in 1911 Huntington sold out to SP, which merged PE with its own interurban lines and continued to expand the PE network as an SP subsidiary. (Henry Huntington's narrow gauge Los Angeles Railway served as L.A.'s city streetcar network and remained independent of both PE and SP control.)

Pacific Electric proclaimed to be the "world's greatest interurban railway" and had the statistics to back it up. At the peak of its operations in the early 1920s, PE operated three districts—northern, southern, and western—that totaled nearly 1,200 route miles with 62 distinct passenger services. Tracks radiated from L.A. as spokes from a hub, connecting many surrounding towns and cities, including Santa Monica, Glendale, Hollywood, Long Beach, San Pedro, Newport Beach, Santa Ana, Fullerton, and Pasadena. Most of the network was electrified at 600 volts direct current, except its high-speed line that extended 58 miles to San Bernardino using 1,200 volts overhead.

Considerable nostalgia has been attached to PE's more esoteric operations, such as its sinuous Alpine Division to Mt. Lowe that PE advertised as the "Greatest Mountain Trolley Trip in the World" (those who never visited Switzerland would be none the wiser). The railway may be best remembered, though, for its extensive passenger routes and intensive operations, such as its Los Angeles–Watts main line, the more prominent of its two quadruple-track lines (a lesser known four-track ran from Valley Junction to El Molino). In downtown Los Angeles, PE operated its own mile-long double-track subway, built at an exceptional cost to remove its cars from crowded city streets.

PE's passenger business was its public face—a face that everyone in the region knew. The company's Red Cars were symbols of L.A. transportation. At its peak in the mid-1920s, and again during World War II, PE accommodated in excess of 100 million passengers annually. Shortly before World War I, it was running thousands of trains daily, including local streetcar services in various communities along its lines.

However, Pacific Electric did more than simply provide transportation for people in existing communities. By design, PE was a vehicle for promoting development, and it essentially created suburbia along its routes. In this way, PE helped pave the way for L.A.'s highway suburbs that developed in its wake.

PE's extensive network also provided Southern Pacific with important freight feeders for its transcontinental traffic. PE supplied SP with perishable traffic—produce from the region's citrus groves that moved in bright-

In this three-way meet on Pacific Electric's four-track line at Watts, a fast-moving car from San Pedro to L.A. overtakes a heavily laden oil train on the outside track. On the left, another freight passes in the opposite direction. Today, this route serves as a Union Pacific freight line and since 1990 as L.A.'s Metro Rail Blue Line. *William K. Barham, Bay Area Electric Railroad Association at the Western Railroad Museum Archive*

It was rare for steam and electrics to work together, but during World War II SP relied on Pacific Electric to help accommodate a flood of freight traffic. This rare image, likely made by F. J. Peterson, shows SP 2-6-0 Class M-7 No. 1740 and PE electric motor No. 1625 working a freight train in the L.A. Basin. *Railroad Museum of Pennsylvania, PHMC*

orange Pacific Fruit Express iced refrigerator cars. Oil was another important source of PE freight traffic. Wells and refineries along its lines were among the most productive in the world in the railroad's heyday. Ironically, the rise of the oil-based highway culture ultimately doomed PE's interurban network.

PE began to feel the pinch of the automobile early, and although the railway's traffic continued to rise through the 1920s, this increase was result of the tremendous population growth in Southern California. In fact, even as PE's traffic grew, its market share declined, and as highway travel became more popular, PE converted its lighter routes to bus services. World War II was the high-water mark for traffic, a result of intensive war-related activity in Southern California combined with serious restrictions on civilian auto travel due to gasoline and tire rationing. When the war ended, PE's passenger ridership and revenues plummeted. By the early 1950s, the railway carried just a fraction of the traffic from a decade earlier. The freeway had gained momentum in L.A. even prior to massive federal investment in the interstate highway system. In 1953, PE

separated its passenger and freight businesses, selling its remaining passenger operations to Metropolitan Coach Lines. Over the next eight years, remaining rail passenger operations were converted to bus. The last former PE line was the heavily traveled L.A.–Long Beach route, which ended service in 1961. The backbone of L.A.'s transportation infrastructure was transformed from an intensive electric rail empire to an intensive road network.

While the Pacific Electric vanished as an integral element of daily passenger transportation, the system continued as a freight railroad. With the end of passenger services, PE converted from overhead electric to diesel-electric operations. When Southern Pacific absorbed the old interurban in 1965, the company was operating roughly 25 percent of its peak route mileage. The system has since been further trimmed, but today PE routes still serve Union Pacific and other freight railroads, while the old L.A.–Long Beach route has been revived as Metro Rail's light-rail Blue Line, and other portions of old PE right-of-way have been incorporated into the L.A. Metrolink suburban rail network.

Pacific Electric's vast electric network once hosted a great variety of freight and passenger services that provided comprehensive transportation in the L.A. Basin. The rise of the automobile gradually killed the system. A Railway Post Office/baggage motor similar to this has been preserved at the Orange Empire Railway Museum at Perris, California. *Bay Area Electric Railroad Association at the Western Railroad Museum Archive*

PART II
FREIGHT OPERATIONS

Freight has long played the most important role in California railroads. Passenger trains might attract the most public attention, but freight has paid the bills. With 5,352 miles of freight railroad, California is ranked by the American Association of Railroads (AAR) as having the third-greatest freight-rail mileage in the United States. It is also one of the most productive states, originating more than 70 million tons of freight and terminating more than 110 million tons annually.

Traditionally, Southern Pacific was the dominant freight railroad in the state, with Santa Fe, Union Pacific, and Western Pacific playing smaller roles. Union Pacific merged with WP in 1982 and then with SP in 1996. The Santa Fe merged with Burlington Northern in 1995, and today Union Pacific and the BNSF are the major players for California freight traffic. In addition, short lines operate dozens of lightly used lines, including those spun off by the larger railroads.

There is no easy path to or through California; the state is famous for its numerous grades. Its mountain lines are familiar names to railroad observers: Donner Pass, Tehachapi, Cajon Pass, and Beaumont Hill are among the best known for railroad drama, while the former WP low-grade Sierra crossing via the Feather River Canyon is known for its rugged scenery and difficult railroad operations because of its volatile geology. There also are plenty of lesser known grades of interest, including the former SP's climb from Dunsmuir to Grass Lake, and the old Western Pacific High Line, known as the Inside Gateway and operated today as the BNSF's Gateway Subdivision. Whole books have been written detailing the history of each of California's famous grades; this section only touches on selected operations.

In the early 1960s, SP F-units in the classic black-widow freight scheme lead a westward freight near Shasta Springs with Mt. Shasta above the train. The former SP route through Dunsmuir and Grass Lake remains a strategic freight line for Union Pacific. Today, the historic Shasta Route is known as the I-5 Corridor. *Bob Morris*

Color in the sky hints of sunset on an otherwise overcast evening as the old guard—BNSF SD40-2s—works east on the former Santa Fe between Stockton and Modesto near Riverbank, California. In contrast with these old goats, most BNSF through freights are hauled by General Electric six-motor diesels with North American Safety Cabs. *Brian Solomon*

This classic image from 1906 depicts a triple-headed SP freight roaring up San Francisco's Harrison Street on the old main line. Prior to the opening of the Bayshore Cutoff, all SP trains left San Francisco on this line. Most traffic was transferred to the Bayshore route in 1907, yet SP's old line via the Bernal Cut survived for a number of years until it was finally truncated and gradually abandoned. *Bay Area Electric Railroad Association at the Western Railroad Museum Archive*

With carload freight, Union Pacific SD70M 3913 rolls northward across the Dry Canyon trestle at Hotlum. The former Southern Pacific Shasta Route remains critical to Union Pacific's I-5 Corridor that handles traffic from the Pacific Northwest. *Justin Tognetti*

A BNSF stack train carrying J. B. Hunt containers waits at Caliente for a descending westbound seen on the upper level of the Caliente horseshoe curve that features a mixed consist of BNSF and Santa Fe GE diesels. The sinuous single-track nature of the former SP in the Tehachapis has been the bane of railroad operations but a boon to photographers. *Elrond Lawrence*

CHAPTER 6

NORTHERN CALIFORNIA

Donner Pass

No main line in California is as old or as formidable as Donner Pass, a difficult mountain crossing named for the ill-fated Donner Party, a group of California-bound settlers whose misfortune found them snowbound on the east slope, resulting in their notorious end. Where Tehachapi, Beaumont, and Cuesta passes are well known among railway enthusiasts, they don't have the popular recognition of Donner.

It was the ascent of the east slope that paralyzed the Donner Party, but it is the west slope—rising from near sea level in Central Valley to the Sierra summit, some 7,000 feet above sea level—that presents the greatest challenge to railroad operations. This brutal 96-mile climb is one of the longest steep grades in the United States. The ruling grade is 2.4 percent, and while the gradient alone would make for difficult running, what really makes Donner difficult is its heavy snow. A heavy winter might dump 50 feet or more on the pass, and at times more than 20 feet of snow covers the ground at the summit. To accommodate such conditions, Central Pacific's builders erected snow sheds. At one time, more than 30 miles of shed extended between Blue Cañon and Andover (west of Truckee on the east slope).

Facing page and above: One of the greatest railroad vistas in California is the view at Old Gorge—otherwise known as "American"—a location east of Alta on the westward ascent of Donner Pass. On a July morning, an eastward Union Pacific freight led by 5922 rounds the bend where rail level is more than 2,000 feet above the American River in the gorge below. *Brian Solomon*

The east slope of Donner Pass provides a dynamic environment to watch climbing freights. Some places are easy to reach from Interstate 80, while others require a little more work. As a thin layer of mist covers the Truckee River, Union Pacific 9542 west roars uphill with autoracks at Polaris, California, 4 miles east of Truckee on UP's Roseville Subdivision. *Justin Tognetti*

A Southern Pacific rotary plow is ready for service at Truckee, California, during a snow squall on February 23, 1993. The rotary's spinning blades are designed to draw snow into the plow and blow it far from the tracks. Although an ancient design, the rotary plow remains one of the most effective tools for moving deep, wet snow. *Brian Solomon*

The development of the Leslie rotary snowplow greatly aided in keeping this vital artery open in the worst weather. But these once-standard snow-fighting weapons have abnormally high operational costs and today are used only in the worst conditions. In modern times, Jordan spreaders, flangers, and smaller equipment such as snow-cats have kept the line clear.

E. H. Harriman's vision brought dramatic improvements to SP's Overland Route, which increased capacity and eased operations. Donner double-tracking was completed in October 1925 (16 years after Harriman's death). At many locations, the second track follows a more modern alignment, with easier grades and curvature, and is not adjacent to the original track. On the west slope, between Rocklin and Colfax, the new line deviates by several miles. This favorable profile required a number of new tunnels, high fills, and deep cuttings. At several places, old and new lines come together at grade or cross one another using grade separations. At Newcastle, the alignments join briefly and the tracks are parallel through a short tunnel before diverging again on different courses through the town of Auburn.

At Donner Pass, there are two crossings, the more recent involving a 2-mile-long tunnel. At Eder, near the east portal of the tunnel, the lines cross and then join again at Shed 47. Since the westward alignment crosses over the eastward line, it results in an unusual example of left-hand running on Donner's east slope. The old line over the summit was last used in 1993 but someday may reopen.

Visions of Donner electrification died with Harriman. In the March 1910 issue of *Railway and Locomotive Engineering*, SP's Julius Kruttschnitt was quoted as saying, "Electrification for mountain traffic does not carry the same appeal that it did two years ago. Oil-burning locomotives are solving the problem very satisfactorily." The oil-burning locomotives of which he spoke were not diesels but rather articulated compounds. Instead of electrification, SP developed its famous cab-forward articulated to work inside Donner's sheds and tunnels, where the combination of long, enclosed spaces and high altitudes made smoke a serious problem. These iconic locomotives were unique to SP.

To make use of powerful Mallet articulated steam locomotives in the Sierra, SP essentially reversed the locomotive. The smokebox faced the tender; both the firebox and a specially designed cab featuring heavy plates to protect the crew were ahead of the boiler. Beginning with new Mallet compounds in 1910, SP's cab-forward design was later adapted for simple articulated types (high-pressure steam to all cylinders).
D. L. Joslyn, T. T. Taber collection, Railroad Museum of Pennsylvania, PHMC

Port traffic has been a growing source of transcontinental railroad business. A pleasant way to view the Port of Oakland, seen here at sunset, is to make the journey on the Oakland–San Francisco ferry from the San Francisco Ferry Building to Jack London Square.
Brian Solomon

Steam was displaced by F-unit diesels in the 1950s, which in turn were replaced by higher horsepower six-motor road switchers in the 1960s. In the early 1970s, SP worked with General Motors on a redesigned airflow scheme to better suit its high-horsepower diesels on Donner. New models, designated SD45T-2 and SD40T-2, rated at 3,600 and 3,000 horsepower, respectively, and known as Tunnel Motors, were a hallmark of the SP's freight operations over Donner for the next 20 years.

The Donner Pass crossing was the most important gateway to California for many years. The route lost its supremacy partly as the result of development of the parallel road network—first U.S. Highway 40, and later Interstate 80. However, by the early 1990s, declines in Bay Area industry, a loss of market share by the Port of Oakland, and changes to perishable shipping eroded the volume of traffic moving over Donner to a trickle.

Railroad enthusiasts have long enjoyed WP's Sierra crossing for its scenery and ease of access. Union Pacific's yellow diesels are easier to photograph in the confines of the canyon than were WP's Perlman green units of the 1970s. This view of UP SD70M 4772 leading an eastward freight on May 10, 2008, was made near a Highway 70 pull-off east of Portola. Alternate angles are available from the old highway below.
Brian Solomon

Donner versus the Feather River

When SP's longtime Overland Route partner, Union Pacific, bought the parallel Western Pacific in 1982, the UP shifted traffic to the Feather River Route. This shift was partly countered when Southern Pacific joined forces with the Denver & Rio Grande Western in 1988. Yet, by that time, the bulk of SP's transcon freight was handled farther south on the Sunset Route. In 1993, SP's under-utilized Overland Route was targeted for cost-cutting and portions of it were single-tracked.

Since UP's purchase of SP, freight traffic has been on the rise. The completion of a fully grade-separated trench in Reno eliminated many grade-level road crossings and ended city-imposed restrictions limiting the number of freights passing over the line. As a condition of the merger, the BNSF Railway was granted limited trackage rights for transcontinental traffic over both of UP's Sierra crossings.

UP sends traffic over both Sierra routes. Where Donner Pass is a shorter, faster crossing with longer sidings and greater track capacity, it suffers from significantly steeper grades. Its 2.4 percent eastward ruling grade requires extra locomotives. In addition, bottlenecks at the Roseville, California, and Sparks, Nevada, terminals, along with heavy snow accumulation, tend to impede operations. Yet, some of Donner's most serious disadvantages are restrictive vertical clearances that prevent the operation of the tallest double-stack trains preferred for domestic container moves.

The former WP Feather River Route features a low-grade profile with a maximum gradient of just 1 percent and enjoys a Sierra crossing that is 2,000 feet lower than Donner and largely free from heavy snow. Union Pacific paid to improve clearances in the canyon in the mid-1980s, and the route can accommodate full-height double stacks. Among the route's drawbacks is the substantially longer distance between Winnemucca, Nevada, and Sacramento. In addition, serious speed restrictions due to tight curvature result in transit times that are six to eight hours longer than the Donner route. Additionally, the WP route is limited because it is entirely single-track (except for the paired track in Nevada) and its sidings tend to be short (by today's standards), limiting maximum train length. Further, the BNSF's Gateway Subdivision freights use the line west of Keddie (to Stockton), adding to congestion in

BIG TRAINS

In modern times, UP has tended to push the limits of train length and tonnage. The largest carload trains might stretch more than 8,500 feet and weigh in excess of 13,000 tons. UP generally routes these rolling monsters over Donner Pass. There, UP has invested heavily in distributed-power technology, which allows the locomotive engineer to remotely control locomotives strategically placed in the middle and at the back of the train. These radio remote-control locomotives are known as distributed power units (DPUs) and take the place of traditional manned helpers. Distributed power aids longer trains by reducing the stress on drawbars and couplers.

In recent years, Union Pacific also has ordered many locomotives using alternating current three-phase traction equipment that delivers extremely high tractive effort at low speeds and can be worked at maximum throttle at low speeds for extended periods without risk of damaging electrical equipment. Eastward, heavy trains have included unit grain trains moving from elevators in the Midwest to the Port of Stockton. Westward, heavy carload trains include the QRVNP-P (Roseville, California, to North Platte-perishables) and, to a lesser extent, QFRNP-P (Fresno to North Platte-perishables). Although designed for perishable traffic, these trains move a variety of carload business. While QFRNP-P fills out at Stockton, where DPUs are added, QRVNP-P is built at Roseville, its DPUs added in the yard. A typical arrangement will see this train operated with two units on the head end, three mid-consist, and two units working at the back.

the canyon. The Feather River Canyon's volatile geology occasionally gets the better of the railroad, and heavy rains can result in serious rock and mud slides. Where snow on Donner can be moved with relative ease, heavy rock slides in the Feather River have closed the route for weeks.

After the UP–SP merger, new track connections were installed at Binney Junction near Marysville (between the WP route and the former SP East Valley main line) and in Sacramento, allowing greater flexibility in UP's routing of through freights. Now intermodal trains can use the Feather River, avoiding congestion caused by Roseville Yard, yet reach Oakland by the more direct Cal-P routing. Alternatively, carload trains using the Feather River Route can serve Roseville.

Owing to the tight horseshoe needed to maintain a 1 percent grade, Western Pacific's 1962 line relocation crosses beneath Highway 70 twice in a short distance at James, east of Oroville. Tight curves and easy road access make James a great place to photograph trains on the Feather River Route. Here, BNSF DPUs catch a glint of light while assigned at the back of an Inland Gateway freight passing James, California. *Brian Solomon*

Facing top: Moments before the sun dips below the rim of the Feather River Canyon, brand-new Union Pacific Evolution-series No. 5357 roars eastward with a double stack across the Rock Creek Bridge. *Brian Solomon*

Facing bottom: On May 23, 1993, Chicago & North Western SD60 7001 leads an eastward American President Line double stack at Virgilia. UP improved clearances on the Feather River Route in the mid-1980s, making it the preferred route for container trains to the Bay Area. On Highway 70 between Oroville and Reno Junction, there are plenty of opportunities to follow and photograph eastward freights in the Feather River Canyon. Here, much of the railroad is limited to 25 miles per hour because of tight curvature. *Brian Solomon*

Right: A Union Pacific freight works the former Western Pacific near Altamont, California, on October 8, 2005. Since 1998, this route has hosted Altamont Commuter Express trains as well as UP's occasional freights. *Philip A. Brahms*

Bottom: Union Pacific SD70Ms 4633 and 5100 lead an eastward freight along the shores of San Pablo Bay at Pinole in the early evening. A short drive from Interstate 80's Appian Way exit is Pinole Shores Regional Park, a popular place to watch trains in the Bay Area. Go north on Appian Way to San Pablo Boulevard, turn left (west) on San Pablo, then right on Pinole Shores Drive. Follow this road to the public parking area at the end of the street. The best views of the line are timetable direction east of the parking area. *Brian Solomon*

Descending the High Line above the Spanish Fork River on the Gateway Subdivision, BNSF 737 west approaches Keddie, California, where it will get a fresh crew. Train symbol PTLLAC3 carries empty trailers from Portland to L.A. and is one of several daily trains that operate via the BNSF's Inside Gateway route. *Travis Berryman*

BNSF's Gateway Subdivision

The 1996 UP–SP merger presented the BNSF with an opportunity to acquire the old WP Inside Gateway between Bieber and Keddie, California, which combined with the railroad's existing trackage and effectively completed a through north–south route from Canada to Mexico.

Today, the former WP Inside Gateway, along with the former Burlington Northern (originally Great Northern) line to Bieber Line Junction at Klamath Falls, is operated as BNSF's Gateway Subdivision. Of the 202 miles between Keddie and Klamath Falls, the first few miles above Keddie are the most visually impressive. There, the railroad crawls away from the narrow defile of the Feather River Canyon. Between Keddie and Moccasin—a 4,208-foot passing siding—track speed is limited to just 12 miles per hour. Freights traveling railroad timetable east (compass north) face a tough 2.2 percent ruling grade between Greenville

and Almanor. Maximum weight for eastward trains is about 5,500 tons. Operations are under track warrant control; the BNSF train dispatcher in Ft. Worth, Texas, issues authority to trains over the radio. The remote and isolated nature of the Inside Gateway is challenging when problems occur.

Traffic on the Inside Gateway ebbs and flows. Traditionally, it has been a corridor for timber products moving from the Pacific Northwest to California markets. Chemicals used in the production of finished timber products travel northward. Most traffic moving via this route is categorized as medium- and high-priority merchandise (carload traffic), but sometimes vehicular traffic and, occasionally, empty intermodal trains use the lines.

By 2005, the Inside Gateway had reached a high-water mark with as many as five trains running in each direction every 24 hours. Since then, traffic via this route has tapered off a bit.

CHAPTER 7

SOUTHERN CALIFORNIA

Transcontinental Dynamics

In the nineteenth century, Los Angeles was considered an inferior natural port compared to San Francisco and San Diego. As result of extensive man-made improvements, however, the ports of Los Angeles and Long Beach flourished to become the most significant in North America. The shift toward containerized shipments that began in the 1950s and accelerated in recent decades has greatly benefited L.A. Today, Los Angeles and Long Beach are the first- and second-largest ports in the United States, respectively (as measured by the number of container units passing through on an annual basis). Combined, they dwarf all other American ports. Thanks to its premier ports and its status as one of America's largest consumer centers, the L.A. area has developed into one of the most significant, if not *the* most significant, railroad freight destinations on the continent. Decades ago, the railroads may have made L.A., but today L.A. makes the railroads.

Growing traffic volumes have been driven in recent years by rapid increases in Far East trade. Railroads carry a significant volume of this traffic and have contributed to the development of the United

Facing page: The Santa Fe crossed the desert from Kingman to Barstow and San Bernardino long before Route 66. Much of historic Route 66 follows the Santa Fe. BNSF 4940 west is framed in Route 66-era ruins near Siberia, California. *Howard Ande*

Above: The Santa Fe's old Bagdad, California, station sign basks in the winter sun. *Brian Solomon*

65

States as a land bridge for goods shipping from the Far East to Europe. Today, the two busiest routes to California are BNSF's former Santa Fe line via Needles and Cajon Pass, and UP's former Southern Pacific Sunset Route. In recent years, both have required unprecedented levels of investment to improve fluidity and increase capacity.

A container is hoisted out of an enormous oceangoing ship. Containers have provided great volumes of railroad freight traffic in recent years. Combined, the ports of Los Angeles and Long Beach form the fifth-largest port complex in the world, having handled close to 16 million TEUs (20-foot equivalent units—the standard measure of containerized cargo) in 2007. Almost half this sum was transported by rail. *Ted Smith-Peterson*

BNSF Transcon

Santa Fe's main line was once the premier passenger raceway from Chicago to California, where streamliners clipped along at 90 miles per hour. The Santa Fe's culture of speed and keeping trains moving translated well into moving transcontinental intermodal traffic. In the streamlined era, railroaders wouldn't dare delay the *Super Chief*, and in the modern one, they wouldn't delay the hot 199 United Parcel Service train, for example.

Since the BNSF merger, the number of trains coming to and from California terminals over the Santa Fe route has more than doubled. Where an estimated 40 trains crossed the Needles Sub daily in 1991, by 2008, as many as 100 trains might use the route daily, making the BNSF transcon one of the busiest freight main lines in North America.

The BNSF's expansive Mojave Desert crossing begins at the Topock Bridge over the Colorado River. The present multiple-span bridge was built in 1945 to replace a previous crossing that was roughly on the alignment of the present highway bridge. The BNSF's double-track bridge is just less than 1,507 feet long and uses a mix of steel-truss and plate-girder spans. A few miles beyond is the desert oasis of Needles, California, an important railroad crew change. Between there and Barstow is the old Santa Fe Needles District, today the BNSF's Needles Subdivision. Equipped with double track since the steam days, many miles have been re-signaled for two-main track operation (bidirectional double track allowing movements in either direction on either track by signal indication) for added flexibility. While not as brutal as other western lines, this route features two long grades. West of Needles, it climbs more than 2,000 feet to Goffs, then drops to Amboy, 614 feet above sea level, before climbing again to Ash Hill. The Ash Hill grade is known for colorful old timetable locations including Bagdad, Klondike, and Siberia. There is a grade separation where eastward and westward lines negotiate separate alignments to allow westward trains an easier climb and eastward trains a more direct route.

At Daggett, UP's Los Angeles & Salt Lake line joins the BNSF's main line; the resulting 9 miles from there to Barstow comprise one of the densest freight routes in California. Barstow is one of the largest terminals on the BNSF, and west of the yard, lines divide, with one route continuing on to Mojave, where the BNSF joins UP's (former SP) route over the Tehachapis; the other line is the busier route, heading toward Los Angeles via Cajon Pass.

Above: The Santa Fe's *Super C* ultrafast intermodal train crosses Cajon Pass. Named after the famous streamliner *Super Chief*, the Chicago–Los Angeles *Super C* was the fastest intermodal train in the United States and operated at passenger train speeds. The Santa Fe discontinued the *Super C* after the railroad lost an important postal contract to the Union Pacific in 1976. *Railroad Museum of Pennsylvania, PHMC*

Left: On March 13, 2007, BNSF 7799 east catches the morning sun while crossing the Mojave Desert at Ludlow. Crews on Bay Area/Central Valley trains work 311 miles from Fresno to Needles, taking them over the Tehachapis and across the Mojave Desert. A priority intermodal train can cross the 168-mile Needles Subdivision between Barstow and Needles, California, in approximately 3 hours 30 minutes. *Howard Ande*

Cajon is the busiest major mountain crossing in California. On September 19, 2003, BNSF 4113 east works its way over Cajon Pass at the famous Sullivans Curve. *Elrond Lawrence*

Cajon Pass

All BNSF trains to the L.A. Basin traverse Cajon Pass—that famous gap in the San Bernardino Mountains surveyed by California Southern's Fred Perris in the 1880s. The east slope of the pass is relatively gentle, but the steeply graded route from the top of the pass, known as "Summit," down the west slope has plagued operations for more 125 years. The Santa Fe made numerous improvements to its Cajon Pass crossing. Prior to World War I, it built a second track on the west slope with an improved alignment that provided a longer but gentler climb. Most westward trains used the old alignment, while eastward trains took the newer one.

Atop the pass, at 3,821 feet above sea level, Summit was a remote telegrapher's office, key to operations in the days before radio and CTC signaling. In 1972, the Santa Fe relocated its line to a slightly lower alignment that reduced curvature, installed CTC signaling to enable trains to proceed on signal indication without orders, and eliminated the Summit office. These changes improved the flow of traffic and increased capacity of the line. In 1967, SP graded its Palmdale Cutoff over Cajon largely parallel to the Santa Fe's line on west slope.

The BNSF's Cajon route remains one of the most difficult transcontinental crossings and has been the site of constant struggles for trains out of the L.A. Basin. In addition to the BNSF traffic, the route hosts Union Pacific trains on the Los Angeles & Salt Lake route. As many as 90 or more trains use the former Santa Fe route daily, with an approximate BNSF/UP ratio of 5 to 1. To cope with traffic growth and expand capacity for the future, the BNSF added 16 miles of third main line between Summit and a point called Baseline, 1 1/2 miles east of San Bernardino. The new track follows the gentle alignment of the eastward track and required the daylighting of two short tunnels. Crossovers between main-line tracks at key locations give dispatchers a high level of operational flexibility in routing traffic over Cajon.

Union Pacific's Sunset Route

Southern Pacific's original main line gradually grew from a secondary transcontinental link to the company's busiest freight main line. The route funnels traffic from New Orleans and Texas to Los Angeles and handles Golden State route business from Chicago and Kansas City moving via Tucumcari, New Mexico, joining the Sunset Route

A warm autumn evening at Sullivans Curve on the BNSF's Cajon Subdivision finds a Union Pacific train rolling down main track No. 1 as another UP train waits in the siding at Canyon. The UP has long reached L.A. via trackage rights over the former Santa Fe's Cajon crossing. Since its 1996 merger with the SP, UP has used two separate routes via Cajon Pass. *Travis Berryman*

at El Paso, Texas. In modern times, the route's capacity constraints have become notorious.

Although largely a single-track route in SP days, the railroad installed CTC signaling in the late 1950s and completed West Colton Yard in 1973. Growth continued, and in the late 1970s, the capacity constraints imposed by single-track sidings encouraged SP to work with American Car & Foundry in designing the first double stack to more efficiently move Los Angeles–Texas–New Orleans container traffic. SP's pioneer double-stack operation began in 1981. It took a few more years before the concept caught on elsewhere, but by the late 1980s, stack trains were common on many American main lines. In the meantime, SP's Sunset Route developed as one of the nation's premier intermodal corridors. Traffic swelled to near saturation by the mid-1990s.

Part of the Sunset Route's difficulty stemmed from single-track operation and acute terminal congestion in Los Angeles and elsewhere, as Union Pacific learned when it inherited the line in 1996. In the following few years, UP operations made headlines as a result of service meltdowns when the railroad simply congealed.

A busy, productive railroad is a good thing, but when a line reaches the limits of capacity—as defined by track space, yard capacity, and availability of crews and locomotives—the whole system begins to break down. A saturated line might seem to offer a steady parade of trains, but that is not necessarily the case in practice. The Sunset Route's capacity constraints resulted in long queues of inbound trains waiting on lonely desert sidings for crews and/or yard space, with outbound trains unable to leave the terminal area for lack of available locomotives and/or crews. This situation was compounded by inadequate siding capacity to make effective meets.

The opening of the grade-separated Alameda Corridor in 2002 greatly improved port access from downtown Los Angeles for both UP and the BNSF, and helped sort out the quagmire west of the Sunset Route. But continued traffic growth kept UP busy trying to meet increased demands on its already saturated main line and at L.A.-area terminals. UP has recognized the need to fund improvements to alleviate bottlenecks, and during the last few years, it has made improvements that SP needed 15 years earlier but didn't have the cash to fund.

As it leaves the L.A. Basin, Union Pacific 4902 leads a stack train and gathers speed east of Hinda near the top of Beaumont Hill. With the urban congestion of L.A. behind it, the train will cross the open deserts of southeastern California, Arizona, and New Mexico. *Travis Berryman*

The west slope of Beaumont Hill has long benefited from sections of two-main track. To increase capacity, UP has connected sidings and laid new track to extended two-main track well down the east slope. Further intensive work is ongoing, and based on a report by Fred Frailey in the November 2007 issue of *Trains,* two-main track ought to extend to the Colorado River by 2010.

The line makes for an interesting study. Although barren compared with Tehachapi and a mere pimple compared with Donner, the Sunset Route's Beaumont Hill has a bit of character and no shortage of traffic. The most scenic portions of the line are east of Colton, where it zigzags its way through San Timoteo Canyon. At the old timetable location known as Apex, the line crests Beaumont Hill (found on maps as San Gorgonio Pass) 2,592 feet above sea level. More open and flanked by Interstate 10 much of the way, Beaumont's east slope offers views of Mount San Jacinto (elevation 10,834 feet) as the line makes a long descent into the desert.

Not only is the Sunset Route the lowest main line in the United States, but it features the longest below-sealevel running anywhere in North America. Originally, the line reached its lowest point 266.5 feet below sea level, crossing the Salton Sink; however, in 1905, the line was flooded as a result of an irrigation scheme gone awry.

When the man-made Colorado River diversion got out of control, it flooded an area 42 miles long and 10 to 16 miles wide, causing the Salton Sink to become known as the Salton Sea. As the water rose, SP was forced to relocate its line several times. Eventually, SP took charge of the situation and, in February 1907, dammed the breach. Today, 39 miles of relocated Sunset Route run to the north of this massive man-made lake.

Despite the curiosity of the low elevation and the history of the Salton Sea, much of the Sunset Route's desert running east of Beaumont Hill to Yuma, Arizona, is unremarkable tangent track. A junction at Niland connects it with the Calexico Subdivision that runs compass south through the Inland Empire to El Centro and Calexico. Traditionally, this connection provided a key link with the San Diego & Arizona Eastern and SP's Inter-California Railway (which offered an alternative south-of-the-border route to Yuma). Yet, the real attraction of the Sunset Route is volume, not natural splendor, although blowing sand and L.A. pollution can make for spectacular sunsets, while enormous wind turbines along the line offer interesting substitutes for trees.

Tehachapi

For Union Pacific and BNSF, Tehachapi presents an enormous operational headache—a strategic bottleneck

The bucolic but rugged nature of the Tehachapis has made it a popular place for watching trains. Union Pacific 4433 east approaches Tunnel 2, railroad direction east of Caliente, on St. Patrick's Day 2002. Southern Pacific's timetable indicated all lines as east-west routes. Regardless of compass direction or actual destination, westward trains were headed toward San Francisco and eastward trains away. This can be confusing for observers in places like the Tehachapis, where curves play havoc with the timetable's relation to the compass. *Howard Ande*

and Bay Area, which in later years saw increasing volumes of intermodal traffic. The route remains critical to the BNSF's strategy, but the pass also serves the railroad's north–south traffic moving via the Inside Gateway route.

Eastbound trains must battle the 2.52 percent ruling grade; by comparison, the westbound ruling grade is a mild 1.36 percent (both figures have been compensated for curvature). The line crests Tehachapi Summit at an elevation 4,025 feet above sea level. In addition to the long, sustained steep grade, the west slope is characterized by numerous tight curves, frequent tunnels, and significant sections of single track that force trains to stop for meets.

In the 1920s, SP built some double-track at Tehachapi to improve traffic flow. It also installed CTC. An earthquake in 1952 and floods in 1983, required substantial rebuilding of the line, and in the mid-1990s, clearances were improved for double-stack trains. Helpers were the rule for many years, although now radio-controlled DPUs are used. Despite these upgrades and improvements, the Tehachapi remains one of the toughest freight crossings in North America. In addition to the famous loop at Walong near Woodford, there are sharp horseshoe curves at Bealville and Caliente.

For photographers, the two sides of Tehachapi offer distinctly different settings. The east slope from Mojave to Tehachapi is a mountain desert, barren and rocky, punctuated by sagebrush and the occasional Joshua tree, and notoriously dry and windy. The west slope is characterized by steeply rolling hills carpeted in rich California grass and marked by an occasional oak tree. Pleasant and bucolic year-round, the area takes on a special character following winter rains, when it becomes a verdant paradise dotted with wild flowers. Although not as busy as Cajon Pass, with better than 40 trains on most days, Tehachapi normally hums with railroad sounds. Busy traffic requires intensive maintenance, and occasionally the railroad is shut for hours at a time to allow track work. Freights queue up on either side of the work and flood the line when the work window is lifted. Pity the crew on a low-priority up-hill train facing five or more opposing moves.

compounded by stiff grades and sections of single track. On the 67 miles between Kern Junction in Bakersfield and Mojave, these two busy railroads share the same line over the pass, making for one of the most heavily traveled single-track mountain crossings in North America.

For railroad enthusiasts, Tehachapi is an almost magical place, thanks to its unique combination of scenery, weather effects, rugged grades, sinuous track alignment, and intense heavy-freight traffic. The scenic splendor of Tehachapi would warrant a visit even if there weren't a railroad here.

The route was engineered and constructed by Southern Pacific. When Santa Fe acquired the San Francisco & San Joaquin Valley Railroad in 1898, it negotiated access to SP's line via trackage rights. For nearly a century, the players remained the same, until Santa Fe became Burlington Northern Santa Fe in 1995 and SP merged with UP in 1996.

Tehachapi is now a key link in Union Pacific's busy north–south routing, described in marketing terms as the "I-5 Corridor" after the roughly parallel interstate highway. (The rebranding of this historic route after a freeway is considered by traditionalists to verge on blasphemy.) For the Santa Fe, the Tehachapi crossing was critical to its east–west transcon route reaching the San Joaquin Valley

CHAPTER 8

SHORT LINES

Today, 3,990 of the 5,352 freight railroad miles in California, and the vast majority of traffic, are handled by the state's two Class I carriers: BNSF and Union Pacific. Yet short lines have had a presence in California since the 1850s, when the state's pioneering Sacramento Valley Railroad built toward Folsom. Twenty-two different short-line railroads carry freight in California today. Some are traditional railroads with long histories, such as the Yreka Western, the Sierra Railroad, and the Santa Maria Valley Railroad, while others are modern creations resulting from Class I spinoffs in the last two decades. The AAR has specific definitions for regional, local, and switching/terminal railroads, all of which are described here by the traditional short-line label. The shortest of these short lines is the 3-mile Quincy Railroad, which connects with UP's former Western Pacific in the Feather River Canyon at Quincy Junction.

Facing page: On May 13, 1981, Santa Maria Valley Railroad 70-ton GE diesels switch Southern Pacific sugar beet racks at the big processing plant at Betteravia in coastal central California. SP's venerable wooden-sided beet racks, complete with old-style journal-box trucks, survived in seasonal service until the early 1990s. Although the cars were eventually replaced by steel hoppers, the sugar beet traffic has now largely dried up due to foreign competition and the increased use of alternative sweeteners. *Brian Jennison*

Above: A common sight for more than 100 years was that of McCloud River Railroad (later McCloud River Railway) freights working east with empties for lumber mills and logging camps. Here, symbol freight MR 37 east works toward the Bartle wye with empties for Burney. It's all just a memory now: economics have changed, and in 2008, McCloud's tracks were being torn up. *Travis Berryman*

Above: California Northern is one of several RailAmerica-owned short lines. It operates three disconnected former Southern Pacific secondary routes, including the West Valley line that runs between Davis and Tehama. SP's West Valley once served as a through route connecting the main Oakland–Sacramento Cal-P line with the Shasta Route. It had been a preferred passenger route because it provided a more direct line between the Bay Area and Oregon. *Brian Solomon*

Left: The Central Oregon & Pacific (known by the initials CORP) assumed operations of SP's Siskiyou Line in July 1995. This line was SP's original main line to Oregon and was renowned for its exceptionally steep grades. Against a backdrop of Mt. Shasta, a CORP local freight works the Siskiyou Line at Weed, California, just a few miles from the junction with Union Pacific at Black Butte. In recent years, high operating costs have threatened viability of through operations via Siskiyou Summit. *Philip A. Brahms*

North America's largest short-line company, Rail-America, has acquired a half-dozen short-line railroads that serve California, largely on trackage spun off by SP and Santa Fe. Its largest California-based railroad is San Joaquin Valley Railroad, which operates 351 miles of noncontiguous line segments in its namesake valley. The next largest is the California Northern (known by the initials CFNR), a railroad that began operations in 1993 on three noncontiguous former SP routes. CFNR serves the former West Valley line between Davis and Tehama—a largely tangent line and once SP's preferred passenger route from

On October 5, 1996, Northwestern Pacific 3844 south crosses a wooden-pile trestle at Comminsky. The historic Northwestern Pacific was formed as joint venture between SP and Santa Fe in 1907, but after 1927 it was solely an SP concern. In 1984, SP began selling off surviving portions of the route, and in 1996, a public agency-funded line was established to operate the historic NWP route from Schellville to Eureka under the Northwestern Pacific name (no corporate connection with SP). This NWP revival was short lived. In 1998, the Federal Railroad Administration shut down the NWP citing safety concerns. As of 2008, the route was dormant, although there have been controversial proposals to re-open revived NWP trackage. *Phil Gosney*

the Bay Area to Oregon; a portion of the West Side line in the San Joaquin Valley between Tracy and Los Banos; and old Cal-P routes west of Fairfield to Vallejo, Schellville, and a connection with the Napa Valley Railroad (host of the Napa Valley Wine Train) near Napa. RailAmerica also operates the Arizona & California, which assumed operations on the Santa Fe route from Cadiz to Phoenix in 1991; the Central Oregon & Pacific, which assumed operations of SP's Siskiyou Line in 1995; the San Diego & Imperial Valley, which provides freight services on portions of the old San Diego & Arizona Eastern route; and the Ventura County Railroad, which interchanges freight with Union Pacific at Oxnard.

Short-line railroading can be a tenuous proposition, especially if a railroad serves just one or two major shippers. Railroads dependant on the timber trade, for example, have been especially susceptible to changes in the economy.

More than one once-prosperous short line has ended operations after the mill it served closed or other changes deprived it of traffic. California Western (see Chapter 14) is an example of a short line that has subsisted on passenger excursion business since its freight traffic ended in the late 1990s. Other lines have not been so fortunate.

For railway enthusiasts, short lines provide a fresh change from the more intense activity of the Class I carriers. Short lines pick up where the big railroads leave off, operating rural branch lines, former secondary main lines, and myriad industrial and terminal trackage. They tend to use colorful (and often antique) locomotives and work at a more relaxed pace. Some short lines may only run once or twice per week but hold to regular operational patterns that can make following a train relatively easy. Other lines operate without frequency or regularity, making it a challenge to catch trains on the line.

PART III
PASSENGER TRAINS

California once enjoyed some of America's finest passenger trains. Old standards such as Southern Pacific/Union Pacific *Overland Limited* (Chicago–Oakland with ferry connections to San Francisco), SP's *Sunset Limited* (San Francisco–Los Angeles–New Orleans), and Santa Fe's *California Limited* were household names in the golden age of railway travel—the early decades of the twentieth century.

The streamliner era began in the mid-1930s as a reaction to traffic lost to highway competition, a situation that was exacerbated by the Great Depression. Streamliners were about style, service, and speed, and the elegant new trains began to reclaim passengers. Southern Pacific's streamlined *Daylight* (San Francisco–Los Angeles) debuted in 1937, spurring a whole family of similar trains. Union Pacific's diesel-powered *City of Los Angeles* (Chicago–L.A.) and *City of San Francisco* (Chicago–L.A. via the Overland Route) were among trains that changed public perception of rail travel. Most famous of all was Santa Fe's *Super Chief* (Chicago–L.A.), operating as a streamliner beginning in 1937. This stainless-steel opulence on wheels set the tone for Santa Fe's fleet of streamlined Budd cars hauled by warbonnet-painted diesels.

California's railroads rallied during World War II, carrying record numbers of passengers. This renewed enthusiasm for passenger travel encouraged the railroads to introduce new streamlined trains after the war. But hopes for a new era of railroad travel proved illusory. Passenger ridership fell off rapidly during the late 1940s and 1950s. Declines continued through the 1960s, as railroads petitioned to discontinue all but a handful of trains. This trend was consistent with passenger train declines nationwide. Financial difficulties with large railroads in the East prompted Congress and the president to provide relief to railroads while preserving a core of long-distance service. The result in 1971 was the National Railroad Passenger Corporation, known by its marketing name, Amtrak.

In its early years, Los Angeles Union Station (LAUS) was known as Los Angeles Union Passenger Terminal and served an estimated 7,000 daily passengers who arrived and departed on long-distance trains, such as Santa Fe's *Super Chief*, UP's *City of Los Angeles*, and SP's various *Daylight*s. Today, LAUS serves 150 weekday trains, largely Metrolink and Amtrak's *Pacific Surfliner. Brian Solomon*

CHAPTER 9

AMTRAK

Amtrak began operations on May 1, 1971, using a ragtag fleet of locomotives and cars inherited from the railroads. Amtrak's red, platinum mist, and blue livery covered over the old names. In California, former SP, UP, and Santa Fe equipment continued to hold down services for a number of years. In the early years, most Amtrak long-distance routes to and from California were accommodated by just one tri-weekly train.

Congress patterned Amtrak as a private corporation, yet failed to consider how the rail-service provider would derive its long-term funding. If private railroads had lost money operating passenger trains, how, exactly, would Amtrak cover its costs? Over most of its system, Amtrak has served as tenant operator, paying host freight railroads for the right to run its passenger trains. Here is the Amtrak paradox: Amtrak is a government-owned operator providing a necessary public transport service over infrastructure largely built, owned, maintained, and operated by private, for-profit companies. By contrast, virtu-

Facing page: Amtrak's *California Zephyr* negotiates the street trackage at Oakland's Jack London Square. In the distance, a Union Pacific freight follows on the other track. It's been nearly 40 years since the classic *California Zephyr* domeliner negotiated Western Pacific's street trackage on Third Street, just two blocks from SP's tracks. WP's train was discontinued in 1970, while its street trackage was abandoned after UP bought SP in the 1990s. Now all trains in the area use the former SP line. *Fred Matthews*

Above: An Amtrak *Pacific Surfliner* car catches the afternoon sun at Fullerton. Served by Metrolink and Amtrak, Fullerton is one of the busiest stations in Southern California. *Brian Solomon*

ally all other transport relies on government-built, -owned, and -maintained infrastructure paid for by taxes (and, in some cases, tolls). Amtrak is the only form of American transport that doesn't have a committed source of funding, such as the highway trust funds.

In the three decades since its birth, Amtrak has relied on federal appropriations to cover its operating deficits and capital-improvement costs. (Provisions were made in Amtrak's charter enabling states to locally fund higher levels of service.) Amtrak's funding has developed into a political football. Its well-publicized funding crises follow cyclical patterns that every few years threaten to kill or curtail services. Despite its inadequate financial structure, Amtrak has survived because of its political nature and continues to provide a skeletal national long-distance network largely along traditional routes established by the railroads during the golden age of passenger travel.

In a few places, Amtrak enjoys substantial state support, allowing it to provide a significantly higher level of service locally than it does on a national level. California enjoys the best intrastate network of Amtrak corridor services as a direct result of statewide publicly supported funding for rail service, including infrastructure improvement and equipment purchases. Nationally, Amtrak is limited by politics, marginal resources for new equipment, and capacity limitations of the freight railroad network it relies upon.

Amtrak Long-Distance Services

California enjoys four Amtrak long-distance routes. These routes are funded and operated as part of Amtrak's national interstate network. Equipment is Amtrak's double-deck Superliners featuring coaches, sleepers, full-service diners, snack cars, and glass-encased observation-lounges.

One of Amtrak's most popular trains is its *Coast Starlight*, connecting Seattle–Portland–Los Angeles via former Southern Pacific routes in California. This train links the historic Shasta and Coast routes at Oakland and offers one of the most scenic journeys in North America. The train is comfortable but not fast, and it provides an extraordinarily pleasant way to travel the length of California, from Mt. Shasta to the L.A. Basin. For many railway enthusiasts and California visitors, the *Coast Starlight* is *the* premier California railway journey operating on a daily basis. Among the scenic highlights are the crossing of the

HIGH-SPEED TRAINS?

Japan pioneered modern high-speed rail when it opened its first Shinkansen line in 1964. This Tokyo–Osaka route hosted the first so-called bullet trains—electrically powered steel-wheel-on-steel-rail trains that traveled initially at a top speed of 135 miles per hour. Over the years, the Shinkansen was improved and expanded, and today Japan operates a nationwide high-speed railway network with top speeds of 186 miles per hour. This system augments a very dense narrow gauge passenger network that runs at more conventional speeds.

France began high-speed rail service in 1981. Top speed in France is now more than 200 miles per hour. Today, many countries across Western Europe enjoy the benefits of high-speed train services, including key international connections, such as the famous Channel Tunnel connecting London with Paris and Brussels. China, South Korea, and Taiwan operate similar high-speed lines, and new routes are planned in Russia, Eastern Europe, and Latin America. Since 2000, Amtrak has operated its *Acela Express* high-speed trains on the Northeast Corridor. These trains can reach 150 miles per hour on short sections of upgraded track between Boston and Washington, D.C. In 2008, California considered construction of a new high-speed route on par with those in Europe and Asia to connect Los Angeles and San Francisco. With cost estimates in the tens of billions of dollars, such a dream is still in the conceptual stages but someday might give Californians the most modern rail transport in North America.

Coast Range by way of the sinuous former SP Cuesta grade between Santa Margarita and San Luis Obispo, and the many miles of Pacific Coast below San Luis Obispo. North (traditional SP timetable direction east) of Sacramento, the *Coast Starlight* tends to run at night, although the Seattle-bound train often passes the majestic, volcanic cone of Mt. Shasta in early morning daylight.

Amtrak's *California Zephyr* connects Chicago and Oakland by way of Denver and Salt Lake City. Amtrak's service uses much of the route of the historic *California Zephyr* between Chicago and Winnemucca, Nevada, but the train should not be confused with the original Budd Domeliner that operated between 1949 and 1970 (see Chapter 4). While the historic *California Zephyr* entered California via Western Pacific, traveling the length of the Feather River Canyon and Altamont Pass, Amtrak's train uses the former Southern Pacific routing over Donner Pass and the Cal-P route between Sacramento

and Oakland. Today, the Feather River Canyon is devoid of regular passenger services. However, the ride over Donner offers another spectacular western journey. It is perhaps best enjoyed after heavy winter storms when snow on the pass can measure more than 10 feet deep and the trees are laden heavily with snow. Donner Pass is a wild and rocky place in the driest of times and a sublime winter wonderland after a Pacific storm. It is no wonder that for many years this line was protected by miles of snow sheds. Today, there are only a few short sheds remaining, yet there are plenty of tunnels on the line, especially at the higher elevations.

It may be something of a surprise, but the old Southern Pacific *Sunset Limited*—a train with a legacy dating to the 1890s—still runs. Before you show up at Los Angeles Union Station expecting a polished 4-4-0, heavily varnished Victorian-era deluxe wooden sleeping cars, and an open-end observation car with brass railings, keep in mind the train has been re-equipped many times since its

The *Coast Starlight* is considered by many Amtrak passengers to be the premier western rail journey. A mix of diesel-electrics leads the train at San Lucas, California, on the former SP Coast Line. Nearly forgotten is SP's economy overnight streamlined coach train from San Francisco to L.A. known as the *Starlight,* which began service in 1949 and was advertised as an overnight "fun train." It departed San Francisco at 8:15 p.m. and arrived in Los Angeles at 6:45 a.m., a significantly faster schedule than offered by Amtrak today. *Elrond Lawrence*

Amtrak's *Coast Starlight* is running a bit behind schedule as it reaches track speed near Dorris in Butte Valley. Northern California passengers eating breakfast can enjoy the stunning view of Mt. Shasta, which may not be possible when the train is on time. *Travis Berryman*

With GENESIS P42s back to back, Amtrak No. 5 glides downgrade at Old Gorge, giving passengers an exceptional view of the American River Canyon. In the nineteenth century, this location was one of several places where Central Pacific stopped transcontinental passenger trains to allow passengers to disembark and take in the view. *Brian Solomon*

beginnings back in 1894. It was absent from the timetable from 1904 to 1911 but was revived after E. H. Harriman's death in 1909. Sadly, SP's luxurious Budd streamlined consists of 1954 are also only a memory. Today, the *Sunset Limited* is run with Superliners, just like Amtrak's other long-distance trains. As one would expect, the train operates over the historic Sunset Route from L.A. to New Orleans—now largely part of the Union Pacific system (although in places, the *Sunset* deviates from the route of SP's historic train). This route is among the busiest freight corridors in the West, and at times it congeals with long trains to and from Los Angeles. The combination of heavy freight and the *Sunset*'s exceptionally long run conspire to throw Amtrak's posted schedules into disarray. It is unfortunate that the name that once conveyed an image of plush travel has come to be synonymous with "delayed." The wise traveler will enjoy the extra time on the railroad. The *Sunset Limited* normally operates in each direction just three times per week (its Amtrak extension from New Orleans to Florida was suspended after Hurricane Katrina in 2005,

and, as of this writing, it is not clear whether service on that route will ever resume).

The BNSF's former Santa Fe L.A.–Chicago transcontinental route hosts Amtrak's *Southwest Chief*, a train still carrying the spirit of the Santa Fe's legendary streamliners. It follows the original route east from Los Angeles via San Bernardino, Cajon Pass, Barstow, and across the Mojave Desert to Needles and beyond. The train's schedule sees the California portion of the run largely covered in the hours of darkness.

Amtrak Corridor Services

Multiple daily departures are necessary to provide successful intercity corridor railway services. This service gives passengers a choice of travel times, alleviates some of the fear associated with missing the train, and facilitates growth and more efficient use of equipment, crews, and facilities. California boasts three of the most successful Amtrak corridors. These, together with an extensive network of dedicated bus feeders and less frequent long-

Led by F59PHi No. 2008 on May 22, 2008, a westward Amtrak *Capitols* service rolls along San Pablo Bay toward its Richmond station stop. On the upper level is a BNSF intermodal train. *Brian Solomon*

On July 19, 1997, Amtrak train No. 715, led by General Electric DASH 8-32BWH No. 2051, and train No. 736, with F59PHi No. 2009 in push mode, pause for station stops at Emeryville. Amtrak California equipment is easily identified by a distinctive paint scheme introduced in 1994 with the first F59PHi. The two Amtrak California GEs are owned by Caltrans and were acquired new in 1992 as part of an Amtrak order for 20 units in the 500 series. They are similar to BNSF's DASH 8-40BWs ordered by the Santa Fe. *Phil Gosney*

distance trains, comprise the most comprehensive, intra-state, intercity, rail-based network in North America.

California's three Amtrak corridors are its pioneering *Pacific Surfliner* route, the San Joaquin Corridor, and the Capitol Corridor. Each of these corridors has historical connections with traditional (pre-Amtrak) services, yet each owes an element of success to California's redefinition and expansion of traditional route structures. California corridor operations are made possible by close cooperation among Amtrak, freight railroads, and local commuter operators, with funding from a variety of federal, state, and local sources.

Pacific Surfliner

The oldest and most successful California corridor operates under the *Pacific Surfliner* brand. It connects San Diego, Los Angeles, Santa Barbara, and San Luis Obispo using distinctively styled double-deck trains. Not only is it the most successful Amtrak route in California, it is Amtrak's most patronized intercity railway route outside the Northeast Corridor in the eastern United States.

Originally known as the *San Diegan* route, the service was inherited from the Santa Fe in 1971. At that time, service essentially consisted of two daily roundtrips between Los Angeles Union Passenger Terminal (LAUPT, since

F59PHi No. 450 leads an Amtrak *Pacific Surfliner* from LAUS to San Diego along the beach at San Clemente Pier on June 1, 2008. The locomotive is designed and painted to match the profile of the bi-level cars. *Brian Solomon*

Back in 1980, with F40PHs hauling Amfleet cars, Amtrak's *San Diegans* looked very much like its Northeast Corridor trains. This train was northward at Oceanside. *Brian Jennison*

Mom and son wait for the *Pacific Surfliner* at the former Santa Fe station in San Diego. For the photographer's son, the thrill of riding the "choo-choo" will not be soon forgotten. *Travis Berryman*

renamed Los Angeles Union Station, or LAUS) and San Diego's Santa Fe station. Historically, this route was a busy line. The October 1949 *Official Guide* lists Santa Fe Table J with four daily limited-stop *San Diegans* in each direction, plus all-stops local trains Nos. 70/75. At that time, the *San Diegan* typically took 2 hours and 45 minutes to make the 128-mile trip.

Amtrak's original pair of services was gradually increased as demand for more frequent service was met with state sponsorship of additional roundtrips. By the early 1980s, Amtrak was operating eight daily trains, more service than the Santa Fe ever had over the route— a landmark achievement in its own right. By the 1980s, North America's halcyon days of railroading were long gone and very few routes enjoyed a level of passenger service even near that once provided by the private railroads, let alone *greater* levels of service.

Success of Amtrak's *San Diegan* route in the 1970s and 1980s led the way for future passenger-rail growth across California. It demonstrated that Californians would indeed ride trains when a good service was offered, while providing an example of successful funding strategies that could be applied elsewhere. Through the 1980s and 1990s, the service was consistently improved. Stations along the line were cleaned up and restored, and

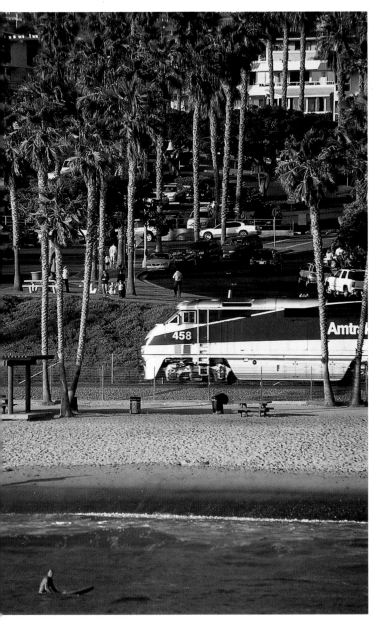

A familiar sight on the Surf Line is that of an F59PHi powering the *Pacific Surfliner*. A few seconds after the train is gone, the surfers and beachgoers will have forgotten about the passage of this northbound train whistling by San Clemente Pier on its way toward Los Angeles. *Ted Smith-Peterson*

service. Amtrak and the state of California bought new equipment from Alstom, including 22 coaches, 17 cab cars, 12 café/coaches, and 10 business-class cars. These cars were painted in the new *Pacific Surfliner* livery and designed to match the profile of F59PHi locomotives, like bi-level "California Cars."

Since the mid-1990s, some *San Diegan/Pacific Surfliner* services have been extended beyond their historic limits and continued up the former Southern Pacific Coast Line, the route also traversed by the *Coast Starlight*. As of 2008, the *Pacific Surfliner* offers 15 roundtrips between San Diego and LAUS, with roughly half of these trains continuing up the Coast Line to Santa Barbara, and two services continuing all the way to San Luis Obispo. It is one of the most pleasant trains to ride in North America, with miles of spectacular views of California beaches and the rolling expanse of the deep blue Pacific—the color mimicked by the train's livery. Passengers can delight in flocks of pelicans gliding above the waves, watch for the occasional breaching dolphin, and admire the skill of surfers as they navigate the currents. Relaxing aboard the *Pacific Surfliner* is much more pleasant than negotiating traffic on the parallel freeways.

The *Pacific Surfliner* connects with various forms of rail and bus transit along its route. At San Diego Santa Fe station and Old Town, the famed San Diego Trolley shares the station with Amtrak and Coaster (see Chapter 11). At Oceanside, four railway services are available, including the new Sprinter (see Chapter 11) to Escondido. Between Oceanside, Los Angeles Union Station, and Oxnard, Amtrak shares stations with Metrolink, and joint ticketing is available. LAUS also offers a variety of rail commuter and transit connections, including the Metro Rail's Red, Purple, and Gold lines.

San Joaquin

Historically, both Southern Pacific and Santa Fe offered through services from the Bay Area to Los Angeles via the broad San Joaquin Valley. Beginning in 1927, this area was the domain of SP's train 51/52, the *San Joaquin Flyer* (later just the *San Joaquin*). The famed *San Joaquin Daylight* service began in 1941 and was later equipped as one of SP's great streamlined trains. SP's *San Joaquin* services operated eastward out of Oakland to Martinez, then via the Mococo line to Tracy and Stockton, and down the valley to Bakersfield. Passengers were afforded views of the Tehachapis as the train wound over the mountains and

in other places new stations and intermodal centers were constructed. Dramatic improvements to this service and other California rail projects were made possible by funds authorized with public ballot initiatives in 1990. In 1994, this funding enabled much of the former Santa Fe route to San Diego to be purchased by public agencies for improved passenger services.

In 2000, the *San Diegan* service was rebranded *Pacific Surfliner*, which helped distinguish it from other California

Amtrak No. 776, a *San Diegan,* makes a station stop at Santa Barbara, California, on August 31, 1998. Renamed the *Pacific Surfliner* in 2000, Amtrak's service has gradually evolved from the Santa Fe's *San Diegans.* Traditionally, trains connected San Diego and Los Angeles via the Santa Fe's Surf Line; today, many trains continue beyond L.A. on former Southern Pacific trackage to Santa Barbara. A few continue all the way to San Luis Obispo. *Phil Gosney*

around the famous loop at Walong to reach Tehachapi Summit. It used the Saugus Line to LAUPT.

The trip over the Tehachapis was scenically sublime and, without question, *the* highlight for the *San Joaquin Daylight* passenger, but the mountain running proved the shortcoming of SP's San Joaquin route. It was longer, slower, and more costly to operate than the Coast Line. SP made up some time with fast running down the valley, yet based on the November 14, 1943, public SP timetable, train 52 (Los Angeles–bound *San Joaquin Daylight*) required 14 hours between terminals (including the ferry ride from San Francisco).

Since the Santa Fe's route between the Bay Area and L.A. was equally tortuous (as it shared SP's route over the Tehachapis) and considerably longer (because it didn't have a direct line from Mojave to L.A.), the railroad didn't bother with a through train. Instead, it offered a bus

connection from L.A. to Bakersfield with its rail service between Bakersfield and Oakland styled as the streamlined *Golden Gate.* The Santa Fe offered the lowest fare in the heavily traveled San Francisco–L.A. market and, in 1939, supplemented the *Golden Gate* with a stylized, steam-hauled, heavyweight train called the *Valley Flyer.*

The Santa Fe's L.A.–Bay Area services succumbed first, while SP's *San Joaquin Daylight* (and the Santa Fe's Chicago–Bay Area *San Francisco Chief*) survived until Amtrak in 1971. Amtrak's national plan didn't include the San Joaquin Valley, which suited SP, which by that time was fed up with passenger trains getting in the way of its freight.

The revival began in 1974, when local interests encouraged an experimental and partially state-funded service called the *San Joaquin.* This service blended portions of the old Southern Pacific and Santa Fe routes. Trains

On a spring evening, an Amtrak GENESIS diesel leads a late-running *San Joaquin* on former Southern Pacific street trackage toward Amtrak's passenger station at Jack London Square. The large numbers of passenger trains and freight movements make the square a great place to watch trains. Area restaurants with trackside views and a direct ferry service to San Francisco are added bonuses. *Brian Solomon*

departed SP's Oakland 16th Street Station and used the SP route via Martinez to Port Chicago, where it joined the Santa Fe and traveled over the Santa Fe lines to Bakersfield. The Tehachapi crossing precluded the train from running all the way to L.A. Instead, passengers reached L.A. via a bus connection.

Initially, the *San Joaquin* was a poor performer. With only one roundtrip daily, trains tended to carry light loads. Although nearly eliminated during budget cuts in 1979, the train survived, in part as a result of the oil crunch that year. Improvements in the early 1980s helped secure the route's future while shaping Amtrak's role in central California. Difficulties with private bus connections led Amtrak to establish its own network of dedicated bus feeders, first on the important Sacramento–Stockton leg, followed by a Bakersfield–L.A. leg about a year later. The success of these bus feeders led Amtrak to develop a complex network of

bus connections for the *San Joaquin* and other California services. Good bus connections, combined with the addition of a second roundtrip in 1980, allowed ridership to grow dramatically.

Improvements have included more effective crew arrangements and better track connections. In its early days, Amtrak relied on the operating crews of its host railroad to run its trains. Crew districts were typically unchanged from the steam era and too often resulted in inefficient modern arrangements. On the *San Joaquin* run, one SP crew was required to bring the train from Oakland to Port Chicago, and then two Santa Fe crews were needed to get it the rest of the way to Bakersfield. In 1980, Amtrak negotiated a simplified crew arrangement and by the end of the decade had further improved matters by hiring its own crews. Another hang-up was the slow and labor-intensive connection between the SP and the Santa Fe at Port Chicago.

EASY TRAINWATCHING: JACK LONDON SQUARE By Fred Matthews

Jack London Square (JLS), at the foot of Broadway in Oakland and adjacent to the Clay Street dock for ferries to San Francisco, is arguably the easiest of all rail-observation locations. There, there are lots of trains in an area where hassling from railroad officials is unlikely—unless you trespass on the fenced right-of-way at the Amtrak depot three blocks southeast (railroad direction east) of Broadway.

JLS offers several good photographing and viewing spots, including the Oak Street crossing east of Amtrak, a pedestrian bridge at the depot, and the famous four blocks of street running between Webster and Clay streets.

JLS is also a visitor-friendly area, offering amazing amenities, including three hotels, a half-dozen restaurants, a huge bookstore with a good selection of rail books and magazines, and even a multiplex cinema if visitors (or their families) tire of trains. Giant container ships no longer loom above onlookers at the square but can be viewed as they are turned and shoved up against the docks just to the west.

If fatigue encroaches, several benches await line Embarcadero West (old First Street). Five of the restaurants there offer good train views, including the bookstore's Starbucks and La Cochina Poblana at Washington Street (both of which have outside terraces), as well as the dinner-only Silk Road next to the tracks at Broadway in the historic Overland Building.

JLS is far busier now than it was a decade ago, as port traffic and especially state-sponsored passenger services have exploded. There are now dozens of scheduled passenger trains on a secondary main that never had more than about 10, plus a dozen or so dead-heads to the new Amtrak shops in West Oakland. Almost all of these trains are four- or five-car push-pull sets of double-deck California Cars, mostly powered by F59PHi units, with Dash 8-BWHs (P32s) and P42s making frequent noisy appearances. The one long train is the 9- to 12-car *Coast Starlight*, sometimes running close to its advertised schedule and sometimes adding or subtracting colorful private varnish.

Freight traffic fluctuates with the economy but remains substantial—roughly 12 to 20 major trains plus a few locals and light engines. Mornings are often heavy, especially before 10 a.m.; afternoons are usually light, except for the BNSF turn between Richmond and Warm Springs with its distinctive nasal horn, and a UP local behind older diesels that roar away from the slow order somewhere between 4 and 7 p.m. The active rail line is two-main track (one for freight, one mostly passenger). A third track has been disused for decades but hosted new streamliners in the 1940s.

When visiting JLS, deep-dyed fans of diesel sounds might consider the economical Jack London Inn on the old First and Broadway station site on Embarcadero West. A quieter and more expensive option is the Waterfront Plaza near the ferry landing, with train sounds in the background and harbor sounds in the foreground. Enjoy!

An SP SW1500 switcher leads a long cut of cars through Oakland's Jack London Square in December 1997. *Fred Matthews*

This is one of 14 dining cars delivered in 1996 for *Capitols* and *San Joaquin* services. A variety of snacks and meals are available, sometimes served with generous doses of wit and commentary. *Brian Solomon*

In 1987, Amtrak paid for the railroads to improve the connection with power crossovers.

The *San Joaquin* used a variety of equipment in its first two decades, beginning with hand-me-down former Union Pacific E-units and SP F-units hauling inherited, decades-old, streamlined passenger cars. Equipment improved over the years, and by 1995 the trains were reequipped with push-pull sets of the new California Cars specifically ordered for Bay Area corridor services. Today, six *San Joaquin* trains operate to and from Bakersfield daily: four from Oakland's Jack London Square and two from Sacramento.

Capitol Corridor

Southern Pacific's line between Oakland and Sacramento had long been one of its busiest and most important routes. This importance was emphasized by the construction of the massive Benicia Bridge over the Carquinez Straits in 1930. The line handled the bulk of Overland and Cascade traffic moving to the Bay Area and was among the few SP routes entirely equipped with directional double track and passing sidings at strategic locations. In its glory days, the line hosted a steady parade of freights and long-distance passenger trains, including the *City of San Francisco, Overland Limited, Shasta Daylight,* and *Cascade.* San Joaquin Valley traffic on the route between Oakland and the junction with the Mococo line (west of

the Benicia Bridge at Martinez) made this section especially busy. In addition to long-distance passenger trains, SP provided San Francisco–Oakland–Sacramento local services. Passengers reached San Francisco via ferries from the palatial Oakland Mole—SP's ancient covered pier extending into San Francisco Bay.

In the 1930s, SP hired Lord & Thomas as consultants to find ways to arrest declines in its passenger service caused by increased automobile ownership and the negative economic effects of the Great Depression. Lord & Thomas were visionary and encouraged SP to buy high-speed, diesel, articulated trains for an intensive San Francisco–Sacramento service. The recommendation was ignored, but had SP acted, these trains might have resembled Germany's contemporary, streamlined, diesel-powered *Flying Hamburger* or perhaps the New Haven Railroad's *Comet* of the late 1930s. Continued losses in the 1940s encouraged SP to scale back Sacramento services, and over the next two decades the railroad fought with the California Public Utilities Commission regarding the levels and quality of service. After 1962, only the long-distance trains remained.

Nearly 30 years after SP effectively abandoned local services on the Oakland–Sacramento route, Amtrak and Caltrans (the state's department of transportation) reintroduced corridor services and even took the service a step further than SP by running trains from Sacramento *through*

Sacramento-bound *Capitols* train No. 538 passes beneath the massive I-80 bridges that span the Carquinez Straits at Crockett. The former SP line between Oakland and Martinez accommodates 40 scheduled passenger trains daily. Intensive passenger operations leave limited windows for Union Pacific freight trains, which now run largely at night. *Elrond Lawrence*

Working in push mode (with the locomotive at the rear), a *Capitols* service glides eastward near Pinole, California, during the early evening of May 22, 2008. Except for Amtrak's long-distance services, virtually all regularly scheduled diesel-powered passenger trains in California use push-pull equipment. *Brian Solomon*

Oakland all the way to San Jose. This extension opened the service to markets never addressed in SP's day. Although discussed for decades, what finally made service possible were 1990 ballot initiatives. The new service debuted with a splash in December 1990. Unlike previous Amtrak trials that began service with a single roundtrip, the new Capitol Corridor was initiated with three roundtrips and plans for rapid expansion. The trains are branded *Capitols* because they connect the present state capitol at Sacramento with the historic state capitol at San Jose.

Amtrak already had infrastructure in place over much of the route. It served stations at Sacramento, Davis, Fairfield-Suisun, Oakland, and San Jose, among other places. It was able to scrounge up spare sets of recently constructed Horizon Cars, a type derived from commuter equipment bought by eastern railroads in the 1970s. Amtrak also obtained necessary cooperation from SP. To expand the service, however, it was necessary to order new equipment. Furthermore, crucial infrastructure improvement was required to allow operation of the 16 roundtrip *Capitols* and the expanded San Joaquin service provided in 2008 (including one roundtrip serving Auburn in the Sierra foothills).

California's commitment to funding statewide passenger services led it to order a distinctive fleet of locomotives to haul its Amtrak-run trains. At a time when Amtrak was looking to General Electric to supply a new fleet of long-distance passenger power, California worked with General Motors' Electro-Motive Division (EMD) to develop a contemporary equivalent to the successful F40PH. To meet California's requirements, EMD adapted its F59PH model to create a modern-looking, streamlined diesel-electric that complied with strict California emission requirements. Designated F59PHi, this locomotive was EMD's first streamlined diesel built for the American market since the last E9 rolled out of its La Grange, Illinois, factory in 1964. Its appearance provided a strong contrast to the utilitarian designs that had prevailed on American railroads since the late 1950s, and it looked very different from GE's recently debuted GENESIS line.

Passenger Train Journal reported that the first nine F59PHi units were ordered by Caltrans in January 1993 at a cost of $20.8 million. Numbered 2001 to 2009 and delivered in 1994, these units were painted in the Amtrak California livery featuring dark blue, gold, and metallic silver. Amtrak received an additional 20 locomotives in 1997, some of which were assigned to *San Diegan* services.

Seen from Pinole Shores Park, Amtrak F59PHi No. 2008 works along San Pablo Bay on a warm May evening. Introduced in 1994, the streamlined F59PHi was the product of input from the California Department of Transportation and the Electro-Motive Division, and it has become the standard locomotive type for Amtrak's California corridor services. The bulbous nose is constructed from fiberglass composite; inside the nose section, steel plates help protect the crew. *Brian Solomon*

Caltrans ordered another six locomotives in the Amtrak California livery; delivered in 2001, these units were numbered 2010 to 2015 and resembled the first order.

Caltrans also bought 66 double-deck push-pull passenger cars from Morrison-Knudsen. (Morrison-Knudsen was reorganized during production, and the order was completed by Amerail.) The cars' styling and profile matches that of the new diesels. Today, these units are standard equipment for both the *Capitols* and *San Joaquin*.

CHAPTER 10

BAY AREA SUBURBAN PASSENGER TRAINS

Caltrain

Today's Caltrain is the most intensive railroad commuter service in California and one of the most intensive diesel passenger services in the United States. The route, which has had continuous passenger service since the San Francisco & San Jose Rail Road opened in 1863, was absorbed by Southern Pacific in 1870 and developed by SP as a suburban passenger line in the 1890s. (The San Francisco–San Jose line was for many years the only commuter line in the West.)

The original route southward from San Francisco (railroad timetable east) was plagued by steep grades and long stretches along the streets through the city. Operationally ineffective, although visually fascinating, this quaint route was bypassed in the early years of the twentieth century. E. H. Harriman authorized construction of the Bayshore Cutoff, a heavily engineered 10-mile line relocation that used a network of major fills and cuts and several long tunnels to shorten and greatly improve the railroad's San Francisco access. Work began in 1904 and was completed by 1907 despite delays caused by the earthquake of 1906. With the Bayshore Cutoff, SP's

Facing page: Caltrain F40PH-2C No. 921, the *San Martin,* leads a San Jose-bound commute. This is one of three new Boise Locomotive machines Caltrain added to its fleet in 1998. The lack of nose-mounted headlights helps distinguish these locomotives from the older F40PH-2s built by the Electro-Motive Division in the 1980s. *Brian Solomon*

Above: The nose section of a Caltrain MP36PH-3C. *Brian Solomon*

line from San Francisco to San Jose was entirely double track, and the new work left provisions for additional tracks. Riders of the line today will notice tunnel portals on the approach to San Francisco built in this period but never used. Interestingly, SP also considered electrifying the line, a concept that is being discussed again more than 100 years after the completion of the cutoff.

In the mid-1950s, the San Francisco–San Jose commutes (a pedantic distinction: while eastern railroads have tended to refer to suburban services as commuter trains, and in modern times the term has worked its way west, SP's peninsula suburban trains were always known as "commutes," a term still appropriate for Caltrain services, despite attempts by the misinformed who insist adding the gratuitous "r") caught the attention of railroad enthusiasts because SP assigned the last of its large passenger steam to the route. This route was among the last intensive applications of big steam power in passenger service in the West. The line regained interest into the 1970s as the last hurrah for SP's distinctive Fairbanks-Morse H24-66

Trainmasters. In 1973, SP's fleet of 20-cylinder SDP45s, bumped from long-distance passenger duties, began to replace the aging Trainmasters, working alongside GP9s and a pair of SD9s.

In 1955, SP supplemented its fleet of Harriman-era commute coaches with new bi-level gallery cars built by Pullman-Standard. An early application of bi-level suburban passenger cars, each was 15 feet 8 inches tall and 85 feet long with capacity for 145 passengers. Additional cars were built by American Car & Foundry.

On May 1, 1971, Amtrak assumed operation of all SP long-distance services, but SP retained operation of the commutes. Amtrak ended long-distance passenger service directly to San Francisco via its Coast Line route, rerouting its sole remaining long-distance train to Los Angeles via Oakland. In the mid-1970s, SP demolished its terminal at Third and Townsend streets in San Francisco. This gorgeous, Mission revival station had been constructed in 1915 for the Panama-Pacific International Exposition. Its replacement was a functional but uninspired intermodal

Caltrain service No. 42 makes a stop at the new Millbrae station. This intermodal center opened in June 2003 in conjunction with the Bay Area Rapid Transit's extensions beyond its longtime terminal at Daly City with a line to San Francisco International Airport and Millbrae.
Phil Gosney

transit terminal a block farther from downtown at Fourth and Townsend streets.

By the late-1970s, SP looked to divest itself of commute train responsibilities. To relieve SP of the financial burden of the service, Caltrans stepped in, providing local funding secured from San Francisco, San Mateo, and San Jose counties. Initially, the trains looked much as they had under SP's stewardship, as the equipment remained the same and SP was contracted as the operator.

Over the next 25 years, the service was transformed by a host of improvements. SP had oriented services entirely toward San Francisco, but in 1981, reverse-commute schedules were reintroduced to serve San Jose in the morning. Another important change was brought about in 1985 when the State of California bought a fleet of new Japanese-built, stainless-steel, bi-level push-pull equipment and 18 F40PH diesel-electrics to replace the aging SP equipment and rebranded the operation as Caltrain. The last of the old cars were withdrawn from service in 1986.

The formation of the Peninsula Corridor Joint Powers Board in 1987 enabled public agencies to acquire the San Francisco–San Jose line along with trackage rights to Gilroy in 1991. In July 1992, Amtrak replaced SP as the contract operator and limited peak-hour services to Gilroy began. With these changes, SP's presence in its home city was limited to the operation of occasional local freights under trackage rights.

Increased highway congestion and significant public demand for rail transit led to further service improvements above and beyond anything imagined in the SP era. Infrastructure improvements begun in 2002 were designed for a substantial service expansion. New passing sidings were constructed at Brisbane (near the deserted former Bayshore Yard) and Sunnyvale with new CTC signaling allowing express trains to overtake stopping trains. New equipment was ordered for express services, and in 2002 the first of 17 Bombardier bi-level commuter cars were debuted. Less than a year later, Caltrain received six new streamlined 3,600-horsepower MP36PH-3C diesels built by MotivePower Industries in Boise, Idaho. In 2004, this new equipment was assigned to the first ten *Baby Bullet* express-train schedules, which reduced transit time from Fourth and Townsend to San Jose Diridon Station from about 1 hour 30 minutes to just under an hour, while increasing line capacity. In 2008, Caltrain was carrying 35,000 passengers on its 96 weekday trains.

Caltrain *Baby Bullet* No. 378 passes Seventh and King streets as it departs San Francisco. Leading is one of six MP36PH-3Cs purchased in 2003. Rated at 3,600 horsepower, these are the most powerful locomotives in the Caltrain fleet and produce a low bass sound at high-throttle positions that can be heard from a considerable distance. It's the next-best sound to SP's SDP45s that worked commutes until the mid-1980s. *Brian Solomon*

This evening lineup of passenger trains at San Jose includes, from left: Caltrain, ACE, and an Amtrak *Capitols.* Convenient connections between rail services and other modes have contributed to the success of California's passenger-rail renaissance. *Brian Solomon*

Locomotive 3102 works at the back of an Altamont Commuter Express commuter train at San Jose, California. ACE provides four weekday roundtrips between Stockton and San Jose by way of the former Western Pacific Altamont Pass crossing. *Brian Solomon*

Altamont Commuter Express

The Bay Area's least-known passenger service is the Altamont Commuter Express (ACE) that runs from Stockton to San Jose via Altamont Pass. ACE service began with two weekday roundtrips in October 1998 and has since expanded to four weekday roundtrips. This limited service was designed to reduce peak-hour highway congestion, giving commuters heading toward San Jose and other Silicon Valley destinations a nonhighway alternative. Trains depart Stockton in the morning and return in the evening. As of 2008, there were no midday trips.

Like other modern California commuter rail services, ACE was the creation of local public agencies. It was originally managed by the Altamont Commuter Express Joint Power Authority (ACEJPA), a group formed by regional agencies for the purpose of providing rail service. This arrangement was refined in 2003, when the ACEJPA was dissolved and the three agencies involved entered into a cooperative agreement. The trains are operated and maintained under contract by Herzog Transit Services.

On the evening of March 6, 2006, Altamont Commuter Express train No. 4 passes Milepost 55 west of Altamont, California, on its way from San Jose to Stockton. ACE trains share this former Western Pacific route with Union Pacific freights. The old SP (former Central Pacific) line that ran parallel to the WP was abandoned in the 1980s, but much of the old right-of-way can still be seen from the train. *Justin Tognetti*

ACE trains use Union Pacific's former Western Pacific route between Stockton and Niles over Altamont Pass. Beyond Niles Canyon, the trains use a former Southern Pacific routing via Centerville and Newark to reach San Jose (shared with Amtrak's *Capitols*). En route, trains serve stations at Lathrop/Manteca, Tracy, Vasco Road (near the famous Lawrence Livermore National Laboratory), Livermore, Pleasanton, Fremont, Great America, and Santa Clara. At San Jose and Santa Clara, passengers can connect with Amtrak and Caltrain.

Crossing Altamont Pass offers a scenic lesson in railroad history. Portions of the parallel Southern Pacific (former Central Pacific) right-of-way abandoned and lifted in the 1980s are still evident. The SP routing was completed in the 1860s, decades before WP's line, and reflects an older standard of construction, with a more sinuous alignment. By contrast, WP's route was built in the early twentieth century using more modern and heavier standards. The two lines crossed at several

locations. In Niles Canyon, the former SP line has been rebuilt for excursion service by the Niles Canyon Railway (see Chapter 14).

Today's ACE routing reflects modern commuting practices. While the old WP line hosted long-distance services such as the famed *California Zephyr* (discontinued in 1970), it had never been a commuter route. Also, WP's passenger trains served Oakland with connections for San Francisco, not San Jose.

ACE uses Bombardier bi-level commuter cars similar to those on Los Angeles Metrolink. As of mid-2008, ACE reported its fleet consisted of nine cab-control cars and 11 coaches. Its locomotives are F40PH-3Cs, an adaptation of Electro-Motive Division's successful GP40-2 and F40PH models but built by MotivePower Industries Boise Locomotive from MK Rail designs. These locomotives are rated at 3,200 horsepower and use an auxiliary engine to send three-phase AC head-end power to the passenger cars.

CHAPTER 11

SOUTHERN CALIFORNIA COMMUTER SERVICES

Metrolink

Los Angeles was a product of railway development. Before the railroad arrived, L.A. was little more than a coastal outpost in an arid basin surrounded by mountains on the edge of a desert. Because of railroad-building and related land speculation in the late nineteenth and early twentieth centuries, Los Angeles flourished and grew at an unprecedented pace. During its early decades, the city's population relied strictly on railways for transport. The region was famous for its extensive Pacific Electric system (see Chapter 5). Later, highways became the chief mode of transport, but railroads remained as freight corridors, and with the growth of the ports at L.A. and Long Beach, transcontinental freight lines swelled with traffic. With the exception of scant Amtrak long-distance services and the *San Diegan* corridor, passenger-rail transport eluded L.A. area residents until the 1990s. In the 1970s and 1980s, L.A. transportation planners occasionally proposed rail transit solutions with little result. In the meantime, as more

Facing page: Halloween 1998 finds an impressive lineup of Metrolink trains at the former Santa Fe station at San Bernardino. Two Metrolink routes serve San Bernardino, including the line named for that city running via former SP and Santa Fe trackage to Los Angeles Union Station and the Inland Empire-Orange County Line that runs via Orange, California, to Oceanside. *Elrond Lawrence*

Above: Air-conditioned cars beckon. Using double-deck commuter trains, Metrolink provides a comfortable, convenient alternative to automobile transport in the L.A. Basin. *Brian Solomon*

freeways were built, traffic congestion grew worse and the air more polluted.

In the February 1993 issue of *Passenger Train Journal*, veteran railway author William D. Middleton pinpointed a key change that helped put L.A. back on tracks: the ballot initiative in 1980 that empowered the recently created Los Angeles County Transportation Commission (LACTC) to begin planning a rail transit system. The measure established funding through a new tax that enabled construction of the L.A.–Long Beach Blue Line, which emulated the recently opened San Diego Trolley while focusing on what had traditionally been one of L.A.'s busiest PE routes. The creation of a heavy rail commuter network was partly an outgrowth of this planning.

It was Southern Pacific that helped push L.A. forward. In 1989, Phil Anschutz (who a year earlier acquired control of SP) endeavored to sell SP trackage in the L.A. Basin to public agencies. This offer presented a remarkable change in attitude by SP. Traditionally, freight railroads had seen government interference as hostile to their operations, and proposals to share track space with passenger trains was met with great resistance. As a major freight carrier, SP in particular had been notoriously hostile to passenger operations since the 1950s. Yet Anschutz recognized that allowing public agencies to assume control of urban trackage for passenger services while freight railroads continued to run tonnage could be a mutually beneficial arrangement.

One attribute of the Metrolink network is distinctive passenger stations owned by local communities. Opened in 1998, Burbank's station features an art deco revival style designed to emulate classic Southern California movie theaters. *Brian Solomon*

Coincident with SP's offer, California voters approved both local and statewide referendums to fund substantial new passenger-rail programs. Not only did the residents of Los Angeles County desire a railway network, but L.A.'s four surrounding counties did as well.

Passenger railroading had moved from control by private companies into the realm of public operations. It was remarkable how quickly various public agencies solved the problems put before them in establishing the Los Angeles commuter rail network. In 1991, the Southern California Regional Rail Authority (SCRRA) was formed as a joint entity of five participating counties. SCRRA negotiated arrangements for the purchase of lines or trackage rights from not just SP, but all three of the major freight railroads serving the L.A. area. The rail service was officially named Metrolink in November 1991, and Amtrak was contracted to operate the service. While Amtrak provided crews and operational know-how, the trains and service are Metrolink's and should not be confused with Amtrak's own services (although there is some service coordination on select routes).

Although the Santa Fe, SP, and Union Pacific agreed to convey trackage and trackage rights, a great deal of infrastructure work was necessary to enable commuter trains to operate on these lines. Passenger trains have different operating requirements than freight trains, and while passenger and freight trains may operate on the same tracks, in order to provide the desired level and quality of service demanded by Metrolink, expensive infrastructure changes were implemented. In some cases, tracks were completely rebuilt. In others, capacity was improved by adding new passing sidings and sections with two-main track (and later three tracks), along with improved signaling. Tracks also were upgraded to allow for smooth running at passenger train speeds (top running speed on some former Santa Fe lines is 90 miles per hour).

Equipment was another important element in the Metrolink equation. Rather than attempt to reinvent the wheel, Metrolink wisely chose to adopt known types of suburban railway equipment. It chose the successful cars and locomotives used in Toronto by GO Transit—a system acknowledged as one of the most effective in North America. This equipment included General Motors' Electro-Motive Division's F59PHs, a road-switcher type featuring the recently introduced wide-nose safety cab. Later, Metrolink bought streamlined F59PHi diesels, which are essentially the same as those used in Amtrak's

California services. Metrolink cars were Bombardier's lentil-shaped bi-levels that offer high-capacity transport while allowing for low-level platforms.

In some cases, Metrolink stations were located at or near traditional station buildings, but in many locations new buildings were constructed. Metrolink was unusual because it encouraged local communities to finance and construct stations along its lines. The most expensive station—and the one most critical to Metrolink's operation—was the historic Los Angeles Union Passenger Terminal, now known as Los Angeles Union Station. This station is the end terminal for most Metrolink services and is by far the busiest station in the network. It serves five Metrolink routes, Amtrak's *Pacific Surfliner* and long-distance services, and Metro Rail's Red Line and Gold Line transit connections.

Metrolink Services

As planned, on October 26, 1992, Metrolink initiated service on three former SP lines, which were branded with new Metrolink route names. Services on SP's Coast Line were branded the Ventura County Line, reflecting the county served at the north (railroad direction west) end of the route. Initially, this route operated only as far as Moorpark but was later extended to Oxnard and Montalvo. The old SP Saugus Line (part of SP's original route to L.A. opened in 1876) was opened to Santa Clarita and thus, along

with related trackage, was named the Santa Clarita Line. In 1994, services were extended all the way to Lancaster. Both of these routes remain as through main lines and host Union Pacific locals and long-distance freights as well as Metrolink. Metrolink's third startup route incorporated portions of SP's Baldwin Park and State Street lines into its San Bernardino Line (initially opened as far as Pomona but soon extended).

The Ventura County Line is also an important Amtrak route for both *Pacific Surfliner* and *Coast Starlight* services. A number of stations are jointly used by Metrolink and Amtrak, and coordinated service called Rail 2 Rail allows Metrolink passengers with monthly tickets to avail of *Pacific Surfliner* services (if these trains are within the limits of their ticket). Likewise, this service enables Amtrak passengers to use Metrolink trains within certain parameters.

Metrolink made consistent progress implementing route and service expansion. In addition to the lines described above, Metrolink's Riverside Line operates over Union Pacific (the former LA&SL route, which predates UP's 1996 acquisition of SP) to the Riverside Downtown station. These services began a few months after the initial startup.

Metrolink also operates three overlapping routes on former Santa Fe trackage. The Orange County Line runs between Oceanside and Union Station, and uses tracks shared with the *Pacific Surfliner* (and open to the Rail 2

On a hot Tuesday evening, a Los Angeles-bound Metrolink train makes a station stop at Fullerton. Metrolink operates the most extensive suburban railroad network in California. Its 2007 statistics indicate it operated 145 weekday trains accommodating an estimated 42,358 riders. *Brian Solomon*

Above, left: In this view looking toward Los Angeles, F59PH No. 860 shoves in the foreground while an F59PHi leading on the approaching train is lost in No. 860's exhaust at Burbank. More than 50 passenger trains pass through Burbank each weekday. *Brian Solomon*

Above, right: The very first train to arrive at Los Angeles Union Passenger Terminal was SP's *Imperial* on the morning of May 7, 1939. The magnificent station suffered from years of decline before being revived in the 1990s. Seventy years after it opened, it is busier than ever. *Brian Solomon*

Rail program). This service began in March 1994. Since 2002, Metrolink's 91 Line has shared the Orange County Line as far as Fullerton, where it continues east on the old Santa Fe Third District via Santa Ana Canyon to the Riverside Downtown station. Because the line also serves as the BNSF's main conduit for transcon traffic heading to L.A. and the ports, much of this route is now equipped with two- and three-main track featuring bidirectional CTC signaling. Metrolink's most unusual route, from the perspective of a commuter rail operation, is the Inland Empire–Orange County Line. Like the 91 Line, this route runs from San Bernardino/Riverside via the old Santa Fe Third District, but it diverges at Atwood (east of Fullerton) to Orange and then down the old Santa Fe Fourth District Surf Line to Oceanside. This route is considered the first modern nonradial commuter service in North America, in that it doesn't serve Metrolink's primary terminal at LAUS. The Inland Empire–Orange County route reflects the travel patterns of many L.A.-area commuters who live and work in the suburbs and have little reason to travel downtown.

Compared with L.A.'s legendary highway congestion and chaos, with multilane freeways notorious for jams at any hour, Metrolink is a traveler's pleasure. The trains are comfortable, clean, climate-controlled, and timely, and riding on the upper level provides a great view.

Coaster

The San Diego area's North County Transit District (NCTD) Coaster trains provide local suburban service on the former Santa Fe Surf Line. Since February 27, 1995, stylish trains painted in aqua blue and white have connected San Diego's old Santa Fe station with Oceanside. The run is 41 miles and serves six intermediate stations. The old Surf Line is shared with Amtrak's *Pacific Surfliner* that provides through services to Los Angeles, as well as with infrequent BNSF freight trains.

Coaster is one component of NCTD's integrated regional public transit system that includes the Sprinter trains to Escondido and Breeze bus services. Coaster connects with Sprinter, Metrolink, and Amtrak's *Pacific Surfliner* at Oceanside. At San Diego and Old Town, Coaster trains connect with *Pacific Surfliner* and the San Diego Trolley. Coaster boasts one of the most scenic commuter runs in the United States. As the name implies, riders are treated to miles of oceanside running.

NCTD reports that Coaster carries approximately 6,000 passengers daily. In 2006, its annual total was estimated at 1.5 million riders. Typically, Coaster runs 144 trains weekly, with 22 trains every weekday. Its modest equipment fleet includes 28 Bombardier bi-level coaches and seven diesel-electric locomotives. Its first five locomotives were

Top: San Diego's Coaster began operations in 1995 to provide local passenger services on the south end of the Surf Line between Oceanside and the Santa Fe's San Diego station. A Saturday evening Coaster glides along the Pacific Coast at Del Mar. *Brian Solomon*

Above: The Coaster works toward Oceanside from San Diego at Del Mar in the evening sun. All Coaster consists use a push-pull configuration with the locomotive facing Oceanside. *Brian Solomon*

Coaster No. 2101 idles at San Diego's old Santa Fe station. The commuter train operator bought five F40PH-3Cs from MK Rail in 1994. These are nearly identical to units acquired a few years later by Altamont Commuter Express and Caltrain from MK Rail's successor, MotivePower Industries' Boise Locomotive subsidiary.
Brian Solomon

F40PH-3Cs, an MK Rail design based on Electro-Motive Division's F40PH and similar to locomotives operated by Altamont Commuter Express. In 2002, Coaster acquired two Electro-Motive Division F59PHi locomotives.

Sprinter

California's newest and most innovative railway operation is the Sprinter service provided by NCTD on the 22-mile former Santa Fe branch line between Oceanside and Escondido. The Sprinter is a bold and unusual application of European-style service and technology in a suburban Southern California environment. Since March 9, 2008, passengers have embraced this well-planned service that makes exceptionally good use of an existing railway right-of-way to provide a frequent, predictable, and affordable rail option on a line previously without railroad passenger services since the 1940s.

In contrast with many startup railroad-based passenger operations that have begun with a handful of peak-period commuter trains time-tailored to meet a target audience, Sprinter began with full, regular-interval service over the length of its run. Trains depart terminals every half hour on weekdays and every hour on weekends, and stop at 15 conveniently located stations along the line. Frequency means passengers need not worry about consulting schedules, which makes it easier to change travel plans without becoming stranded because of gaps in the timetable.

There are many benefits to interval-service operations. Over the long term, it helps to build service, especially during off-peak travel times. While regular-interval branch-line operations are standard in many European countries, they are relatively unusual in the United States.

In common with European railway services, Sprinter connects to a larger network of public transportation: the trains serve intermodal centers with regional buses and at Oceanside connect with Amtrak, Metrolink, and Coaster trains. In this way, Sprinter acts as a feeder to other rail services. This approach benefits riders taking longer journeys and makes it convenient and desirable to leave automobiles at home. With an across-the-platform transfer at Oceanside, Sprinter passengers can travel by rail to downtown San Diego, Los Angeles, Riverside, and Santa Barbara, as well as a host of intermediate stations.

Not only is Sprinter a regular and convenient service, but it's comfortable as well. Sprinter trains are a variation on the modern Desiro model—a standard diesel multiple unit (DMU) built by Siemens AG. Large numbers of these trains operate in local passenger service on main line and branch lines in a number of European countries, including Germany, Austria, and Slovenia. Each Desiro is a streamlined two-piece articulated railcar. NCTD bought VG642 models, which are powered by a pair of 420-horsepower turbocharged, intercooled, six-cylinder diesel engines.

Unlike most American diesel locomotives, which use some form of diesel-electric transmission, the Desiros have a five-speed torque converter. Because of the multiple-unit connections, a single engineer may operate several VG642 Desiros coupled together, allowing for longer trains during peak travel periods. The trains have a top design speed of 55 miles per hour. While this speed is not considered high speed for a modern railway, it is more than adequate for service where there is barely a mile between most stations. Rapid acceleration is as important as a high operating speed.

Above: California's newest passenger service is the Oceanside-to-Escondido Sprinter using Siemens-built diesel multiple units similar to those used in many European countries. The former Santa Fe branch was built in 1887 by the California Central Railroad, and until Sprinter, Escondido had not hosted regular passenger services since the late 1940s.
Brian Solomon

Left: Low floor sections give easy access to mobility-impaired Sprinter passengers and eliminate the need for building expensive high-level platforms.
Brian Solomon

Key to the Desiro's success is its multiple low-floor entrances. This design enables passengers to board trains quickly without assistance from train staff and makes it easier for handicapped passengers to use the trains without need for special equipment or prolonged station stops. Sprinter's Desiros are maintained at a modern shop facility near the Escondido Station toward the eastern end of the line.

In Europe, Desiros and other lightweight modern railcars are standard equipment on many railway lines, routinely operated alongside heavy passenger and freight trains. However, as a result of different signaling and safety requirements in the United States, stricter and more restrictive procedures are required for operating lightweight railcars on tracks shared with freight trains. As in the case of the San Diego Trolley and other light-rail operations, Sprinter and freight trains can only share the tracks using a system of temporal separation—that is, separation in time—that guarantees when passenger trains are on the tracks no freight trains are operating, and vice versa. Because Sprinter operates between the hours of 4 a.m. and 9 p.m., no freight trains can use the tracks at those times.

Also of operational interest is a section of line used only by Sprinter. This largely elevated, grade-separated line features unusually steep grades and was built for Sprinter to access Cal State University's San Marcos station. Freight trains continue to use the traditional Santa Fe alignment, which is shorter and features gentler grades than the new elevated passenger alignment.

CHAPTER 12

SAN FRANCISCO MUNICIPAL RAILWAY

According to published figures, San Francisco's Municipal Railway accommodates an estimated 700,000 passengers daily using various transit modes, including cable cars, light-rail streetcars, and various modes of rubber-tire transport. Its world-famous cable cars have undoubtedly made the "Muni" the most familiar of all California's rail transport systems, though today they represent only a small part of the network. Few may realize that these rolling San Francisco icons were once operated by private companies, and when Muni inherited the cable operations in the 1940s and 1950s, it viewed these classic transit routes as antiquated impediments to progress and sought to abandon them. San Franciscans fought hard to retain the cable cars from total abandonment, and they have become major tourist attractions, as well as everyday transit links for lucky residents.

Cable Cars

In the formative years of railroad-building, railroad engineers routinely used cable haulage where steep grades made it impractical for conventional locomotive-hauled trains. Known as inclined planes,

Facing page: This panned view captures the motion of a San Francisco Municipal Powell & Hyde cable car on its way toward Market Street as it rolls down Washington. The ability to ride standing on the outside of the car remains one of the great thrills of the San Francisco cable car experience. *Brian Solomon*

Above: Detail of the front of Muni PCC No. 1057. *Brian Solomon*

San Francisco cable cars survive as an active part of the Muni network. Here, a grip man does his thing as cars pass on Hyde Street. In the case of cable cars, peak periods have little to do with conventional commuter patterns, but, rather, when tourists arrive. Residents use the cable cars when they are not swamped with tourists. The passengers on this car are regulars traveling with a monthly Fast Pass. Visitors must pay higher cash fares that are more expensive than other Muni routes. *Brian Solomon*

Facing page: San Francisco Muni Cable Car No. 20 grinds along Mason Street toward Hyde. *Brian Solomon*

these grades required stationary steam engines to move cars with cables. The most extensive and famous inclined planes were those used on the Allegheny Portage Railroad over Pennsylvania's mountains.

Although cable-hauled railways had been around for decades, the innovation of the commercial cable-hauled streetcar is credited to British-born Andrew Smith Hallidie. In 1841, German immigrant John Roebling introduced metal-wire cable as an improvement over traditional hemp cables. This new material made for more reliable operations, and by the 1860s, Hallidie began manufacturing wire cables in San Francisco. The city was undergoing rapid transformation from a remote military outpost to a bustling urban center, and transporting people through the streets was becoming increasingly important. Horse cars had been a popular innovation in many American cities, and in the 1860s, San Francisco had several horse-car routes. But the technology was impaired because city planners had imposed a linear street grid irrespective of topography, resulting in many viciously steep thoroughfares.

Melding several key cable innovations, Hallidie established San Francisco's Clay Street Hill Railroad in 1873, considered the first commercially successful cable-hauled street railway. It set a number of precedents that precipitated a revolution in urban transport, and it was copied not only in San Francisco, but in nearly 30 cities across the United States and around the world. Hallidie's prototype railroad was very short. It extended just 2,791 feet but ascended 307 feet on a maximum gradient of more than 16.2 percent (consider that the Central Pacific's ruling grade on Donner Pass was 2.4 percent). This railway was a narrow gauge operation—3 feet 6 inches between inside flanges—and a central conduit between the rails carried the cable. The cars reached the cable using a grip that extended through an open slot in the street surface. Important to this system was development of a variable grip that allowed the controlling grip man to alter the speed of the cable car in stages while the cable operated at a constant speed. With this system, the cars could stop at various points along the line, working uphill faster than other street railway systems.

Above: In 1885, before San Francisco embraced the electric streetcar, horse cars and cable cars congregated at the foot of Market Street in front of the old Ferry Building. *Railroad Museum of Pennsylvania, PHMC*

Right: This circa-1953 photograph shows a California Street Muni car climbing west at Grant Street. Until the 1950s, the California Street line extended across Van Ness Avenue into the Western Addition. In the mid-1950s, Muni truncated the line at Van Ness, while melding portions of the old Hyde Street trackage with the former Washington & Jackson and Powell & Mason routes to form a new hybrid cable car route known as the Powell & Hyde line. *Fred Matthews*

The Clay Street Hill Railroad's financial success resulted in several other companies extending cable car lines across San Francisco. The last new route opened along O'Farrell, Jones, and Hyde streets in 1891.

At the peak of the cable car boom in San Francisco, a half-dozen private companies operated cars on lines with a variety of track gauges. Market Street Cable Railway operated one of the most extensive cable car networks. The company evolved from a horse-car line and was among the San Francisco street railroads owned, controlled, or otherwise influenced by the famous Big Four. In addition to its Market Street trunk line were lines on Hayes, Haight, McAllister/Fulton, Valencia, and Castro streets.

The cable car's reign as the dominant streetcar system was cut short by Frank Sprague's development of electric streetcar—or trolley—technology in the 1880s. Because of its hills, San Francisco initially was slower than other cities to adopt the trolley car on a large scale, but following the devastation of the 1906 earthquake and fire, the city made a rapid switch to electric operation. A few cable car routes survived, and as late as the early 1940s, there were a number of cable car lines operated by two private companies.

Muni inherited the old Ferries & Cliff House and Powell & Mason routes in 1944 when it took control of the Market Street Railway. Then in 1951, Muni absorbed the routes of bankrupt California Street Cable Railroad,

Car No. 12 works the Powell & Hyde route as it crests Hyde Street on Russian Hill with Alcatraz visible in the distance. Every day, cable cars ascend San Francisco's steep hills on grades exceeding 20 percent. San Francisco's steepest transit routes are handled by buses—the 67 route to Bernal Heights climbs a grade slightly steeper than 23 percent. *Brian Solomon*

A cable car ascends Nob Hill. The sights and sounds of the cable cars are intrinsic to San Francisco. Today, it seems bizarre that in the 1940s the city's mayor proposed getting rid of the remaining cable car routes because they didn't mesh with his ideas of progress.
Fred Matthews

including the public utilities commission, considered them expensive and outmoded. The public disagreed. People loved the cable cars, and the citizens of San Francisco were not going to allow misguided modern opinions destroy one of the city's icons. A *San Francisco Chronicle* editorial on February 3, 1947, echoed the popular perspective: "It is rarely that persons who have visited San Francisco discuss it without mentioning the cable cars, and very rarely that this mention is anything but favorable...."

Yet, Muni succeeded in truncating remaining cable car operations, and angry protests occurred when lines were closed. In May 1954, on the eve of the O'Farrell, Jones & Hyde route closure, an anonymous individual made front page news by threatening the new mayor if the cars ceased operation. Closure went forward, and the line was shut after 63 years of service. Two years later, the Washington & Jackson line was discontinued.

Complete closure was politically sensitive, so Muni compro-

giving it five distinct cable car routes operated as two separate systems. Muni was keen to convert cable cars to buses, reflecting the attitude of San Francisco's transit planners who had made clear since the 1940s their intentions to abandon surviving cable cars. Postwar planners and politicians viewed cable cars as anachronistic and impediments to rubber-tired vehicles. In 1947, Mayor Roger D. Lapham was famously quoted as favoring buses, describing cable cars as "dangerous and costly." Other transportation progressives,

mised by blending lines and retaining a scaled-back system that remains today. Muni's three surviving cable car routes have just 4.7 miles of trackage, far less than what it inherited and a fraction of the pre-1906 earthquake network.

In the early 1980s, the surviving cable car infrastructure was deemed life-expired. There was no question the network system was worn out. Service was routinely interrupted when the cable broke—the familiar whirring sound below the street would stop without warning and

Time was running out for the O'Farrell, Jones & Hyde Street cable car. This February 1954 image shows the final Jones Street "Dinkey." Full-sized cars lasted another week before the line was closed. *Fred Matthews*

cars would grind to a halt. Repairs could take hours. Again, the system faced oblivion, but the decision was made to reinvest in the cable cars. In 1983 and 1984, the entire system was closed while the trackage and conduits were dug up and rebuilt, and the combined powerhouse/car barn was totally rebuilt. Although the structure's exterior was retained, virtually all of the working equipment inside the powerhouse was replaced. Bits of the old cable have been sold as souvenirs. Though a few replicas are operated alongside the historic cars, the majority of the operating cable cars are authentic—many now more than 100 years old—and all have been thoroughly rebuilt.

Above: Visitors line up to board cable cars at the corner of Powell and Market streets. This Powell & Hyde car is about to be turned in May 1966. *Richard Jay Solomon*

Left: Cable car No. 23, heavily laden with tourists, climbs Jackson Street on the run from Powell and Market to Hyde and Beach streets. The Powell & Hyde route was a 1950s amalgamation of several earlier routes traditionally operated by different companies. *Brian Solomon*

Facing page top: Muni No. 1063 catches the setting sun on the Embarcadero. Historically, trackage on this alignment was operated by the freight-hauling San Francisco Belt Line. *Brian Solomon*

Facing page bottom: A J Line car works west along Market Street in 1957. Muni's tracks for the defunct Geary Street line can be seen diverging to the left. At the time, the Hobart Building (on the left) was one of the tallest structures in San Francisco. *Fred Matthews*

Streetcars

City transport in San Francisco—as in all American cities—was originally the domain of privately operated companies that planned, built, and operated transit lines for profit. Companies competed for passengers, and routes were built where the most money could be earned. In cable car days, routes often ran along a single street. Over time, companies were consolidated into larger systems. The largest in San Francisco was the Market Street Railway, which, during its long, complicated, and multimodal history, used a variety of operating names. It started in horse-car days as the Market Street Railroad, later operated as the Market Street Cable Railway, and for a few years was the United Railroads of San Francisco (reflecting consolidation of a variety of smaller lines). Finally, in its last years from 1918 to 1944, it was known as the Market Street Railway.

The first publicly operated transit line in the United States was the San Francisco Municipal Railway, established in 1912 to operate the Geary Street line. Since Muni's inception, virtually every transit operation in North America has made the transition from private company to public agency.

Muni changed the way transit routes were planned, establishing new routes to create transit corridors designed to develop new areas of the city. Later, as private companies in San Francisco faltered as a result of rising labor costs and increased ownership of private automobiles, Muni assumed operation of city transit routes.

Muni PCC No. 1062 dressed in Louisville, Kentucky, paint works Market Street at California Street. Historic PCC cars acquired from Philadelphia in the 1990s are an important part of the F Line fleet. Each is painted in a different livery to represent a city that once used PCCs. The concept is popular, although many visitors confuse the representative paint schemes with the car's heritage. The Market Street Railway maintains its own museum at the Steuart Street car stop on the F Line near the Ferry Building—now called the Ferry Plaza. *Brian Solomon*

Muni's early expansion included new lines to serve the city's Panama-Pacific International Exposition held near Fort Mason in 1915. A related improvement was the Stockton Street Tunnel built to serve a new streetcar line and road traffic. Today, the tunnel remains an important corridor, although the streetcar line was converted to buses decades ago. Muni's later and lasting improvements included the 1915–1916 construction of the new J Church Line to help encourage development in the outer

Mission District. This route features private right-of-way though Mission Dolores Park. In addition to developing the Sunset District beyond Twin Peaks—San Francisco's most imposing topographic feature—Muni bored an 11,920-foot tunnel. The east portal is on Market Street near Castro, while the other end is in the region of the city that became known, appropriately, as West Portal. When the tunnel was completed in 1918, it initially served Muni's K Ingleside Line. The L Taraval (originally part of a Market Street Railway route) and the M Ocean lines were added later.

Market Street is San Francisco's most important thoroughfare. Before Muni, it was served by Market Street Railway, which was not keen on sharing its already busy lines when Muni wanted to expand. So in 1918, Muni constructed its own parallel tracks along the length of Market Street, resulting in a rare example of a four-track street railway. Market Street Railway used the inside tracks, while latecomer Muni used the outside tracks. At rush hour, this route was the busiest street railway in the country, with most cars turning at the Ferry Building, where large numbers of commuters accessed boats.

Muni continued to invest in new trolley lines after electric railways began their decline nationally. Muni's last major expansion of the period was construction of the Sunset Tunnel, finished in 1928, to host the N Judah Line, named for the Central Pacific's Theodore D. Judah. This route left Market Street with the J Church Line at Duboce Avenue and served the western suburbs beyond the tunnel along Carl, Irving, and Judah streets.

In 1944, Muni took control of the Market Street Railway, the city's largest streetcar operator. Between the late 1930s and the early 1950s, Muni was transformed as a result of this acquisition and crucial changes in regional transport stemming from the opening of the trans-bay bridges and a modal shift from rail-based to rubber-tire transport. Muni relocated its streetcar tracks toward the new Trans Bay terminal (located several blocks south and west of the ferry terminal) to reflect the decline of the once-important Ferry Building. Acquisition of the Market Street Railway produced a blend of the two intertwined systems, and Muni introduced a new green and cream livery to reflect consolidation of San Francisco's transport.

Above: Traditionally, Muni and the Market Street Railway had turn-back loops at the Ferry Building. Today, tracks from Market Street use a dog-leg arrangement to join the alignment once used by the San Francisco Belt that takes cars toward Fisherman's Wharf. Here, former Philadelphia PCC 1056—dressed in the colors of the Kansas City Public Service—rolls in front of the Ferry Building on a May morning. The car was built in 1948 and is one of more than two dozen historic PCCs (Electric Railway Presidents' Conference Committee streetcars) in San Francisco. *Brian Solomon*

Left: Dressed in Muni's pre-1944 blue and gold livery, No. 1010 is one of three smooth-riding, double-ended PCCs in historic F Line service. The F Line extension has contributed to the redevelopment of the waterfront, in part made possible by demolition of the elevated Embarcadero Freeway after the 1989 earthquake. The historic cars are advertised as "Museums in Motion" and are among of the most enjoyable railway experiences in modern San Francisco. *Brian Solomon*

Market Street Railway had suffered from years of neglect, so after World War II Muni modernized the private railway's former routes by converting most to electrically powered trolley buses. Muni had identified its routes with letter codes, while the Market Street Railway used numbered routes. These differences were roughly translated into the present coding whereby letters are used for streetcar lines and numbers for bus routes. Today, many low-numbered bus routes still reflect routes and route numbers of former Market Street Railway streetcar lines. After the war, Muni pared back its own streetcar trackage, and even its pioneering Geary Street routes were converted to buses in 1956. Reducing the number of streetcars on Market Street allowed Muni to remove two of the four tracks in the late 1940s.

Muni invested in a fleet of new and secondhand Electric Railway Presidents' Conference Committee (PCC) streetcars during the 1940s and 1950s, which served until the early 1980s. (The committee was formed in 1929 by presidents of various electric railways to devise a new streetcar to help fend off automobile and bus transport.) A handful of Muni's original PCCs survive today in historic F Line service alongside secondhand PCCs acquired from eastern cities in the 1990s.

Muni Metro

Muni never completely abandoned its streetcars. Surviving routes—the J, K, L, M, and N lines—represented a core system that largely benefited from the tunnels and private rights-of-way developed in the 1910s and 1920s. When the new Bay Area Rapid Transit (BART) system was planned in the 1960s, provision was made for a Market Street trolley subway to run one level above the BART tracks. Muni's subway connected with its Twin Peaks Tunnel at Castro. BART began service along Market Street in 1973, but the Muni Metro took a few more years to use its subway.

This 1971 view of Market Street was made during BART subway construction when shoo-flies were necessary to keep Muni streetcars rolling. At this time, PCCs were the rule on Muni and were assigned to the J, K, L, M, and N routes. Note the Union Pacific building on the far side of the street. Many of the buildings pictured here have since been replaced with modern skyscrapers. *Fred Matthews*

Above: A BART train glides along on a reinforced-concrete elevated structure in West Oakland. Below, an Amtrak F59PHi and California Cars are washed for Capitol Corridor service. Since this December 19, 1998, image was taken, the tracks used by Amtrak were removed to make way for a new Union Pacific yard. *Phil Gosney*

Left: With evening sun and fog making for a cosmic setting, BART trains pass at Rockridge Station. The train on the left is bound for Concord. Envisioned as completely redesigned rapid transit, the BART features nonstandard specifications aimed at overcoming traditional shortcomings. For example, it uses 5-foot-6-inch gauge to provide greater stability for lightweight trains running at nominally high speeds. *Fred Matthews*

In conjunction with Muni Metro, Muni ordered its first new streetcars in decades. Its PCCs ordered in 1952 were the last streetcars built by a traditional American company. Lack of advancement in North American streetcar design from established U.S. manufacturers led San Francisco and Boston to award a joint order for modern streetcars to Boeing-Vertol, a new transit car subsidiary of the well-known aircraft manufacturer. In a bit of political spin, these transit cars were designated "light-rail vehicles" (LRVs) to differentiate the new cars from the antiquated-sounding trolley cars they were to replace. The first LRV was delivered to San Francisco for testing some 25 years after the last new PCC had arrived for service. Over the next few years, Muni completely reequipped its fleet.

The Muni Metro opened for service in phases. The old PCCs were not suitable for subway service, so they continued to work the surface lines while LRVs were phased in on subway services. In February 1980, N Judah was the first line to use LRVs exclusively. The last traditional Muni PCC operations were concluded in 1982. From that time onward, the five principle streetcar lines served the Muni Metro subway. The Market Street trackage was without regular service, and for the next dozen years this once-key streetcar route saw operations only on special occasions. Tracks were removed between Duboce and Castro (although a link to the Twin Peaks Tunnel was retained via trackage on Church and 17th streets).

Modern Expansion and Historic F Line Trolleys

In the last three decades, Muni significantly expanded its streetcar network with extensions and new routes. With the opening of the Muni Metro, it extended the K Ingleside Line to Balboa Park, thus giving better access to the car barns near this terminal. In the early 1990s, the J Church Line was also extended by way of San Jose Avenue to Balboa Park, allowing better system interconnection.

Market Street trackage was the venue for the Historic Trolley Festival in 1983 while the city's cable car system was rehabilitated. Vintage streetcars from San Francisco

Muni PCC No. 1061 in Pacific Electric colors is seen in front of the Ferry Building. In its heyday, this building was one of the most heavily used transport hubs in the world. *Brian Solomon*

and cities around the world provided daily service to the delight of visitors and railway enthusiasts. This festival demonstrated the popularity of operating streetcars on Market Street and represented the first steps toward developing the Market Street route as a historic streetcar line. In the 1980s and early 1990s, a nonprofit group using the historic Market Street Railway name operated streetcars on special occasions.

Car No. 1893 has finished for the day and approaches the Geneva Street car house on San Jose Avenue. Popular with visitors, it is one of eleven Peter Witt–style cars imported from Milan, Italy, for historic services on Muni. All were built in 1928 based on an American design.
Brian Solomon

The F Line began service in 1995 following restoration of Market Street trackage to Castro Street and Muni's acquisition of former Philadelphia PCC cars that were rehabilitated to as-new condition. These cars are brightly painted in the liveries of various American transit systems to commemorate the wide role the PCC played in twentieth-century American transit. In addition, the F Line operates a number of historic trolleys, including a fleet of imported Peter Witt–style cars from Milan, Italy (this style was designed by and named after a 1920s-era Cleveland Railway commissioner). In 2000, the F Line was extended along the Embarcadero to a turn-back loop near the popular attractions at Fisherman's Wharf, a few blocks from the Powell & Mason cable car terminus.

A more recent Muni expansion includes extension of the Muni Metro beyond the Embarcadero Station to a new street portal near Folsom Street and street trackage to the Caltrain commute station at Fourth Street, where N Judah services now terminate. In June 2007, Muni opened its new 5.1-mile T Line streetcar route from a junction near the Caltrain station to Sunnydale (near the old Southern Pacific Bay Shore Yards) along Third Street. As in the 1920s, when new lines were built to develop new areas of San Francisco, this line was opened with visions of revitalizing some the toughest parts of the city. T Line services feed into the Muni Metro subway. Beware: by no means should the T Line be confused with the F Line service aimed at the tourist trade.

The old San Francisco Belt Railroad was a short line that served the San Francisco waterfront. Although portions of the old Belt Line were still in place into the early 1990s, by that time the railroad no longer played a substantive role in freight transport. Today, Muni's F Line uses new trackage on the old Belt alignment. Notice the dual-gauge tracks that allowed the Belt to accommodate narrow gauge cars from the North Pacific Coast and other regional lines that arrived by ferry for local delivery or transloading. *Bay Area Electric Railroad Association at the Western Railroad Museum Archive*

In recent years, Muni has added several prominent extensions to its streetcar network. Among the most heavily utilized is the line from the tunnel portal at Folsom along the Embarcadero to the Caltrain station. On a bright October morning, one of the modern Breda light-rail vehicles on the N Judah run works toward the Caltrain station. *Brian Solomon*

A southward Muni Breda streetcar is in T Line service on Third Street near Gene Friend Way. The route opened in 2007 and is Muni's newest rail line. *Brian Solomon*

CHAPTER 13

CALIFORNIA'S LIGHT-RAIL REVOLUTION

The American light-rail revival was sparked with the opening of the San Diego Trolley in 1981. San Diego rediscovered the virtues of electric streetcars as a means of providing cost-effective, rail-based transport over the city's lightly used freight lines. By the 1970s, most American cities had abandoned traditional streetcar services, and only a handful of cities, such as San Francisco, retained portions of their old streetcar networks. Although such electrically operated rail networks are often known as light-rail systems today, they embrace many of the essential qualities of the old electric street railway and trolley car. San Diego acknowledged these historic connections by calling its new system the San Diego Trolley.

San Diego Trolley

Key to the development of the San Diego Trolley was the San Diego & Arizona Eastern (SD&AE), a Southern Pacific affiliate that had once provided San Diego with a transcontinental link to the Sunset Route by way of Mexico and the Carrizo Gorge. In

Facing page: San Diego Trolley U2 cars at the Santa Fe station in downtown San Diego. An Amtrak *Pacific Surfliner* trainset is visible in the distance at left. *Brian Solomon*

Above: S70 low-floor cars built by Siemens for the San Diego Trolley are assigned to Green Line service, a 19.3-mile route that operates over the Mission Valley extension between Old Town and the Santee Transit Center. *Brian Solomon*

A San Diego Trolley Orange Line car approaches America Plaza on West "C" Street in downtown San Diego. Nos. 2001–2052, all models SD100, were built by Siemens in San Diego and are one of three varieties of light-rail vehicles used by the San Diego Trolley. These cars are relatively angular in appearance, compared with the original U2 cars. *Brian Solomon*

San Diego Trolley Siemens-Düwag U2 streetcars pause at America Plaza near the Santa Fe station. *Elrond Lawrence*

1976, washouts caused by Hurricane Kathleen severed the line as a through route (although local freights continued to serve portions of the line). It took a few years, but closure of SD&AE had set the stage for new development. When SP opted to divest, the city of San Diego acquired portions of the line and the city's Metropolitan Transit System created its San Diego Trolley subsidiary to operate and maintain the route.

In its early days, the San Diego Trolley was largely a single-track operation made possible by stringing wire over upgraded former SD&AE tracks. Service began in summer 1981. New bright-red Siemens-Düwag U2 electric cars plied the rails from downtown San Diego 16 miles to San Ysidro, across the U.S.-Mexico border from Tijuana. To maintain freight services on the line while the San Diego Trolley uses the same tracks, a system of temporal separation was designed wherein freight trains and trolleys use the tracks at different times to ensure that there is no possibility of collision between light-weight light-rail cars and heavyweight freight locomotives and trains.

The San Diego Trolley was an extremely successful operation from its start. Not only did it encourage expansion of the system, but it encouraged other cities in California and across the United States to consider light rail as a modern transport solution. By 1984, much of the San Ysidro route (originally known as the South Line and today as a component of San Diego's Blue Line) had been equipped with directional double track that allowed for faster and more frequent service. An extension eastward

Top: The San Diego Trolley's newest route is its Mission Valley Line (now operated as its Green Line), seen in this view at the Qualcomm Stadium Station. *Fred Matthews*

Above: A Los Angeles Metro Rail Blue Line train negotiates street trackage in Long Beach on part of a large single-track balloon through the downtown area. The modern Blue Line runs along much of the former Pacific Electric L.A.-Watts-Long Beach route. *Brian Solomon*

over the former SD&AE branch to Santee was opened to Euclid Station in 1986. Originally, this was known as the San Diego Trolley's East Line, and it is now a component of the Orange Line, which runs 20.7 miles from downtown San Diego to Gillespie Field, while the Blue Line was extended 3 miles from downtown to Old Town in 1997.

The San Diego Trolley's most modern route is operated as its Green Line, which is 19.3 miles long and includes the highly engineered Mission Valley Extension that opened in July 2005. This all-new and largely grade-separated extension includes long sections of reinforced-concrete elevated structure and San Diego's first subway, contrasting sharply with the quickly converted railroad lines that characterized the San Diego Trolley's early operations.

The San Diego Trolley offers excellent system connectivity, allowing for fluid operations and ease of passenger transfer. The east end of the Green Line shares a portion of its route with the Orange Line, while the Orange Line and Blue Line overlap in downtown San Diego. The Blue and Green lines meet at Old Town with occasional Blue Line service continuing east over the Green Line route as far as Qualcomm Stadium Station. The system's track network can be envisioned as a gigantic figure 8 with a long southward Blue Line tail to San Ysidro and a short northeastward Green Line tail to the Santee Transit Center. At both the Santa Fe station in downtown San Diego and at Old Town, the San Diego Trolley provides cross-platform connections with Amtrak and Coaster services.

In late 2008, San Diego was planning a historic streetcar route called the Silver Line patterned after San Francisco's successful F Line. Silver Line service will be provided by a nonprofit subsidiary of the Metropolitan Transit District. It is expected this line will use a pair of restored PCC cars with San Francisco Muni heritage but acquired from a third party. The Silver Line is expected to operate in a loop on existing downtown trackage shared with the Blue and Orange lines.

Los Angeles Metro Rail

In July 1990, a decade after San Diego paved the way for modern light-rail transit, Los Angeles Metro Rail opened its first new light-rail route. The L.A.–Long Beach Blue Line was the beginning of the region's passenger-rail revival. Significantly, it re-established rail transit that largely followed the old, formerly four-track Pacific Electric right-of-way to Long Beach. Although the last passenger services on the PE line were discontinued in 1961, the Southern Pacific still used the old PE line for freight when the Blue Line tracks were constructed parallel to it. (This arrangement remains today, although SP's successor, Union Pacific, provides the freight service.)

Since its opening, the Blue Line has developed into a heavily traveled north–south corridor. Visitors planning to ride this line should be aware that the route passes through reputed L.A. gang lands.

L.A.'s Green Line light rail was in the planning stages when Blue Line construction began in 1987; Green Line service began in 1995. Today, this 20-mile east–west line runs from Norwalk to Redondo Beach, with a

Top: Portions of Los Angeles Metro Rail's 13.7-mile Gold Line light rail use the former Santa Fe Second District through Pasadena. This route opened in July 2003. In this June 2008 view, one of L.A.'s new Breda-built light-rail cars assigned to the Gold Line is destined for Los Angeles Union Station. These cars have stainless-steel sides with gray-painted fronts that present a very different appearance than other types of Metro Rail LRVs. *Brian Solomon*

Above: Sacramento's Regional Transit Blue Line light rail is seen near the Florin Road station, south of downtown Sacramento. The former Western Pacific main line is parallel to the light rail's flyover for Florin Road. RT riders are occasionally entertained by the passing of long freights. *Brian Solomon*

passenger transfer to the Blue Line at the Imperial-Wilmington station and shuttle bus connections to Los Angeles International Airport (LAX) from the Green Line's Aviation/LAX stop. Although passengers can transfer between the light-rail lines (Imperial-Wilmington is one station north of Compton on the Blue Line), the two routes are grade-separated and isolated from one another; there are no track connections.

The most recent L.A. light-rail route is its Gold Line, which runs directly from platforms 1 and 2 at Los Angeles Union Station to Sierra Madre Villa station in Pasadena. This line operates on a modern reinforced-concrete elevated alignment from LAUS through Chinatown; after crossing the channelized Los Angeles River, it joins the alignment of the former Santa Fe Second District (once that railroad's premier passenger route to L.A.). The Gold Line's heritage is evident in places—the former Santa Fe Pasadena station is still adjacent to the line. Gold Line service began in January 2003, and as of 2008, the Gold Line was 13.7 miles long with extensions planned. The route was conceived as an extension of the Blue Line, but this extension never developed, and as with Metro Rail's other routes, the Green Line is physically isolated.

Back in Pacific Electric days, Los Angeles had a short trolley subway. Since 1993, L.A. has again enjoyed the benefits of conventional underground (heavy) rapid transit with the opening of its Red Line subway (LAUS to North Hollywood). The Purple Line extension of the subway to Wilshire Boulevard and Western Avenue has since opened, giving Metro Rail five rail transit routes. Passenger connections can be made with the Gold Line at LAUS and with the Blue Line at Metro Center. All Metro Rail routes provide clean and reliable rail-based transit service.

Sacramento Light Rail

Regional Transit, Sacramento's bus provider, began modern light-rail services in 1987 on an 18.3-mile, partially single-track, L-shaped route. This line connected a large park-and-ride facility along Interstate 80 at Watts Avenue (northeast of the city) with downtown, and then turned due east, running to a terminal at Butterfield Avenue. In most places, single-track sections were gradually replaced with double track. Since 1998, the system has had several extensions that have produced a reconfigured route structure. Now with 37.4 track miles, Regional Transit's light rail serves 47 stations on two routes; each route is made up, in part, from the original system, and they overlap through downtown.

The Blue Line runs on a north–south alignment from the I-80/Watts Avenue station to Meadowview Station in South Sacramento. The southern portion of this route runs parallel to Union Pacific's former Western Pacific main line, with Regional Transit's LRVs often running alongside UP and BNSF freights (the latter use the WP line via trackage rights stemming from the 1996 Union Pacific–Southern Pacific merger).

Regional Transit's Gold Line runs westward from historic Folsom toward downtown, following the route

of California's first railroad, the Sacramento Valley, with the light-rail line terminating at the Amtrak station using a short stub-end line completed in 2006. In downtown, the lines run within sight of the state capitol building and feature some interesting street trackage while traversing the K Street pedestrian mall. As of 2008, Regional Transit had a fleet of 76 LRVs. The older cars are Siemens U2A designs assembled locally. Trains routinely run up to four cars long.

San Jose and Silicon Valley

One of the least remarked-upon modern railway networks in California is the Santa Clara Valley Transportation Authority's light-rail system. Initial operations began in 1987 and as of 2008 consisted of a 42.5-route-mile network with three lines connecting downtown San Jose with regional suburbs and office parks. Intermodal connections are afforded with Caltrain, ACE, and Amtrak at the San Jose Station; with Caltrain at Mountain View; and with ACE at Santa Clara's Lick Mill station. Much of the line is suburban in character, with tracks generally located in the center median of multilane roads, serving office complexes, shopping centers, and regional housing. In downtown San Jose, tracks are in the street and serve a downtown pedestrian mall. After about 15 years of service, the original light-rail fleet was replaced with new cars to better serve mobility-impaired passengers.

Above: Sacramento's Regional Transit light-rail U2A cars were built locally by Siemens. In downtown, the light-rail system includes some interesting street running, as well as trackage through the pedestrian areas of the Capitol Mall. *Brian Solomon*

Left: San Jose's light-rail system serves suburban sprawl characterized by modern office complexes typically associated with highway-dependant development. This LRV car at Calle del Sol is destined for Mountain View and is about to cross over the former SP line near the Great America station. *Brian Solomon*

PART IV
RAILWAY MUSEUMS AND EXCURSIONS

California is host to a great variety of railway museums and excursion lines. Some, such as the Orange Empire Railway Museum, have roots dating back more than a half century. Others are more recent creations. Preservation covers virtually every aspect of California railway history, from its formative beginnings in the 1850s to relatively modern second-generation diesels. Long-passed operations such as electric interurban lines and narrow gauge common carriers are remembered by railway preservation. Museums, meanwhile, house a great variety of locomotives, cars, and artifacts, while excursions provide visitors with an opportunity to experience period equipment at work, often in scenic settings. Railway preservation remains an ongoing effort, and many museums rely on visitors and patrons to help fund projects, while volunteers of all ages donate their time to making their railway dreams—and the railway dreams of others—come true.

Yreka Western 2-8-2 No.19 is seen with Mt. Shasta in the distance. The Yreka Western is a Northern California short line that has augmented its nominal freight business with seasonal passenger excursions. On rare occasions, it has been known to haul freight with steam when its diesels are inoperative. *Fred Matthews*

CHAPTER 14

DIVERSE PRESERVATION

Niles Canyon Railway

Less than an hour's drive from San Francisco is the Niles Canyon Railway, one of California's best active preserved railway lines. Volunteers from the Pacific Locomotive Association have re-laid nearly 10 miles of former Southern Pacific line in the narrow defile of Niles Canyon, while providing a home for dozens of preserved locomotives and railroad cars. This scenic setting, characteristic of SP in California, was part of Central Pacific's original 1869 all-rail route to the Bay Area. Although eclipsed by other routes, it survived as a secondary freight route until 1984 when it was abandoned and later lifted.

Since the late 1980s, Niles Canyon volunteers have been slowly rebuilding the railway. Their reconstructed line has the characteristic hardware of an SP secondary main line from the steam-to-diesel transition period. Grade crossings are protected by classic wigwag-style automatic flagmen manufactured by the Magnetic Signal Company of Los Angeles (a

Facing page: It's hard to beat the draw of a live steam locomotive working upgrade. Fans line up on the Niles Canyon Railway to photograph SP No. 2472 running east at Brightside. *Brian Solomon*

Above: Among the most attractive Pacific types were SP's powerful, well-balanced Class P-8s built by Baldwin in 1921. Several have been preserved, and on this May 2008 morning, restored No. 2472 attracts a big crowd at Niles Canyon Railway's Sunol station. The handsome locomotive has thrilled thousands in excursion service since 1991. Its sister, P-8 No. 2467, also restored in the 1990s, briefly worked excursions but is now displayed at the California State Railroad Museum in Sacramento. *Brian Solomon*

Southern Pacific P-8 No. 2472 climbs through Niles Canyon with an excursion train in May 2008. SP's Pacific types were standard mainline passenger power in the 1920s and 1930s. The P-8s survived to the end of steam, working in secondary services, and were retired in the 1950s. No. 2472 is one of several survivors. It was restored to service in 1991 in time for Sacramento Railfair '91, where it made its public debut. *Brian Solomon*

The Niles Canyon Railway re-creates an atmosphere of 1950s California. Here, restored GP9 No. 5623 in the black-widow livery leads an excursion past Vallejo Mill near Niles, California. *Brian Solomon*

standard type of grade crossing signal before the common adoption of flashing red lights). Classic Union Switch & Signal lower-quadrant semaphores are positioned line-side. These signals were once standard automatic-block protection across the SP system. (On the Niles Canyon line, signals are not yet tied into a functioning automatic-block system but add a nice touch to the setting.) At Sunol, the former SP 1880s-era passenger station is dressed in the classic mustard and brown paint scheme that adorned SP structures system-wide.

The Pacific Locomotive Association collection is stored at the Brightside Yard, a couple of miles down the canyon from Sunol. Among the many first-generation diesels preserved there are several former SP units, including GP9

Built by Pullman in 1911, Southern Pacific coach No. 1949 is typical of Harriman-style all-steel cars assigned by SP to San Francisco and San Jose commutes. Today, it adds to the authenticity of period excursions operated by the Niles Canyon Railway.
Brian Solomon

No. 5623 built by General Motors in 1955 and restored in the as-built black-widow livery. Western Pacific fans also will be happy to see F7A No. 918D with its shiny bull-dog nose. This unit is one of the final four Western Pacific F-units operated through Niles Canyon on the former WP main line parallel to the old SP route (on the opposite side of the canyon). Several small steam locomotives have been preserved there, as well. In 2008, celebrity steam locomotive Southern Pacific No. 2472, a Baldwin-built heavy Pacific, made appearances on excursion trains. It was a fine sight that attracted thousands of visitors.

Passengers are regularly afforded excursions over the line between Sunol and Niles Station in Fremont. Generally, excursion trains are made up of heavyweight cars typical of SP and its affiliated lines. The result makes for very convincing period trains in an appropriate setting. It's hard to beat!

Roaring Camp and Big Trees

In the Santa Cruz Mountains near Felton is Roaring Camp, a period attraction that serves as a railroad-themed park and heritage area. Of interest are its two railroad operations. One is a standard gauge former Southern Pacific branch operated by the Santa Cruz, Big Trees & Pacific. It serves as both a freight-hauling short line and a passenger excursion operation. Excursions are operated between Felton and the Santa Cruz boardwalk using a former Santa Fe CF7 diesel passing through a redwood forest on its way to the coast. This line is a short remnant of the historic South Pacific Coast (SPC), a fantastic narrow gauge line known for its difficult engineering and built between Dumbarton Point (on the lower portion of San Francisco Bay), Newark, San Jose, and Santa Cruz over the spine of the Santa Cruz Mountains. The SPC's completion ceremony at Big Trees on May 15, 1880, was famously marred by a serious fatal derailment, while the railroad's planned celebration of its conversion to standard gauge coincided perfectly with the earthquake of 1906 (by that time, it was part of the SP empire). Through service over the mountains ended in 1940.

The other operation is the Roaring Camp & Big Trees (RC&BT), a re-created line built in the 1960s that emulates the steeply graded, timber-hauling, narrow gauge lines common in Northern California during the early twentieth century. This line begins with a balloon track at Roaring Camp and follows a sinuous, very steep route that winds among coastal redwood trees on its ascent of Bear

Mountain. Passengers are treated to splendid views of enormous ancient trees as the logging locomotive labors to climb the mountain. The route includes a curved trestle, a switchback with 10 percent grade (built in 1976 to bypass a burned corkscrew trestle), and a second balloon track at the top of the hill. RC&BT has two active Shays and a Heisler—two varieties of geared steam locomotives used for heavy, slow-speed service on lightly built track.

The RC&BT is one of the few opportunities in the Bay Area to see live steam locomotives running year-round. It runs most weekends with seasonal weekday trips. Commentary provided during the trip is informative and includes a detailed explanation of the Westinghouse air-brake, crucial technology used in modern railroading and obviously necessary for the return trip from Bear Mountain to Roaring Camp.

California Western

A through railroad was never built along the Northern California coast. This vast area of sparse population and difficult terrain couldn't have supported such a line. Even the railways that grew to comprise the Northwestern Pacific (NWP) stayed inland. The coastal mountains were famous for majestic redwood forests, with their coastal sequoias having grown for thousands of years and ranking as the world's tallest living things. Largely untouched

Above: Built in the 1960s, the Roaring Camp & Big Trees is a narrow gauge railroad re-creation emulating the spirit of steep sinuous lines once used to extract timber from Northern California forests. It makes for a splendid ride among the redwoods near Felton. *Fred Matthews*

Left: The California Western is famous for its gas cars. Car No. 300 is a streamlined skunk train, long popular with tourists and railroad enthusiasts. The California Western cars earned the nickname for their characteristic exhaust odor. This view is at Willits, California, the railroad's east end, where it traditionally interchanged with Southern Pacific's Northwestern Pacific subsidiary. *Brian Jennison*

by man until the mid-nineteenth century, these massive redwoods—up to 375 feet tall and 23 feet in diameter at their base—seemed out of scale with all else. Where some people were awed by the sublime beauty of the redwoods, others saw unrivaled opportunity—a commodity to be harvested and money to be made.

The old military outpost of Fort Bragg was conveniently located where Pudding Creek and the Noyo River emptied into the Pacific. In 1885, the Fort Bragg Railroad was built to connect timber mills and timber stands along Pudding Creek. In 1891, various smaller lumber companies were consolidated as the Union Lumber Company, which also controlled the railroad. In its early days, this isolated railroad was akin with the various lumber railroads constructed elsewhere across Northern California.

To better serve timber stands in the upper Noyo Valley, the railroad bored a 1,184-foot tunnel under the ridge that separates the Pudding Creek and Noyo River watersheds. The railroad gradually pushed eastward and, in 1905, was renamed the California Western Railroad & Navigation Company (CW), which reflected the company's modes of moving timber. The railroad's business flourished following the massive earthquake and fire in April 1906 that devastated much of San Francisco and surrounding communities. Redwood was in great demand for the next few decades as San Francisco was rebuilt. The colorful gingerbread houses that characterize the city are partly a result of redwood's characteristic building qualities.

The railroad pushed its line over the Coast Range to Willits using a tortuous route with numerous reverse curves and a second tunnel (its summit is 1,740 feet above sea level). In December 1911, the line reached Willits, where the CW met the Northwestern Pacific. The opening of the CW as a through route coincided with the railroad's maturity from strictly a timber hauler to a commercial carrier. In 1912, it introduced a regularly scheduled passenger service over the length of its main line. Soon, the railroad was attracting visitors to the region who came to witness the splendor of the forests and the atmosphere of Fort Bragg. For a few years in the 1920s, a through sleeping-car service was scheduled between Fort Bragg and the Bay Area over the CW and NWP.

As with many branch railways, a low-cost passenger service arrived in the form of petroleum-powered railcars. Self-propelled railcars were much lighter than conventional trains and used only a fraction of the fuel to provide the same service. California Western purchased its

When gasoline-powered railcars were new back in the 1920s, people accustomed to the aroma of steam locomotives thought the cars smelled like a skunk. The name stuck, and the California Western has thrived for years as "the route of the skunk train." *Brian Jennison*

first railcar in 1925, a railbus built by Mack. A second car was acquired a decade later. Railcars were a quirky contrast to traditional steam locomotive–hauled trains; they were a blend of highway and railway technologies that generated considerable interest with the traveling public. Where most railcars had run their last miles by the 1950s, CW's not only survived, they made the railroad famous. For years, CW operations have been popularly known as the "skunk train," because of the smell of the railcars' emissions. A stylized smiling skunk wearing an engineer's cap serves as the line's mascot.

Into the 1970s, the California Western still carried significant freight traffic, using Baldwin diesels to move approximately 7,000 cars of timber and forest products annually. Freights were typically nocturnal, connecting with the NWP at Willits. Changes in the economy and the nature of transport in the region gradually eroded the railroad's freight traffic, however, and by the 1990s, CW transported only a few hundred cars annually. In 1998, the Federal Railroad Administration shut down the NWP for safety reasons, a move that isolated CW from the rest of the national railroad network. The same year, the timber mill in Fort Bragg closed.

As freight traffic declined, the railroad's role as an excursion line became more important. Its passenger service had evolved from traditional scheduled trains serving communities along the line into primarily day excursions for tourists. In 2008, seasonal excursions were offered from both Fort Bragg and Willits. At times, these excursions still operate with vintage railcars but also may use locomotive-hauled consists. Due to the relatively remote nature of the line, before making the long trip to visit there, it's best to inquire with the railroad to ensure trains are operating.

Western Pacific Railroad Museum

The moderately sized Western Pacific was an underdog in the transcontinental business; every step of the way, it vied with the giant Southern Pacific for territory and traffic. Yet its quirky existence, spectacular Feather River Canyon, and friendly crews made it a favorite of railroad enthusiasts.

The famed Budd-streamlined *California Zephyr* had been one of the best known trains in the West. WP operated vintage Electro-Motive F-units in freight service into the 1970s—longer than any other California carrier. The railroad was absorbed by Union Pacific in 1982, which preserved its route structure and ensured greater levels of traffic than when WP was independent. Still, WP's fans mourned the loss of the railroad's colorful character.

The Feather River Rail Society (FRRS) was formed in 1983 to help keep the spirit of WP alive. Today, the FRRS operates a 37-acre museum and 2 1/2 miles of track adjacent to the former Western Pacific yards at Portola, California. Part of the site includes WP's 1954-built diesel shop. The Western Pacific Railroad Museum (WPRM) has become home to more than 30 first- and second-generation preserved diesel locomotives, along with dozens of freight and passenger cars. Many of the locomotives are authentic former Western Pacific machines. Two of its famous F-units, including No. 805A, a rare FP7A model used in *California Zephyr* service, reside there.

Enthusiasts of early diesel power will enjoy a visit to the Western Pacific Museum at Portola and its wonderful array of preserved WP first- and second-generation diesels, as well as models from Southern Pacific, Union Pacific, and other western railroads. *Brian Solomon*

Western Pacific's first diesel, old SW1 No. 501 has its place among the more recent models, which include several Electro-Motive GP models and examples from General Electric's Universal line. Among the museum's most cherished pieces is former 0-6-0 steam switcher No. 165, which was built by Alco in 1919 and worked on the WP between 1927 and 1953. In late 2008, this rare surviving example of WP steam was undergoing restoration that may see it eventually return to operating condition.

Although focused on WP, the museum has preserved a variety of equipment from other western lines as well, displaying locomotives from Southern Pacific, Union Pacific, and regional short lines. These locomotives include the massive UP Centennial diesel No. 6946—EMD model DDA40X built in 1969—the largest and most powerful single-unit diesel-electric ever built. For a few years in the early 1980s, these monsters were regular visitors to former WP rails.

On select weekends, the WPRM operates its preserved diesels for the public. If you are aching to hear a classic 567C diesel under load, the WPRM is a great opportunity! The museum also offers instruction in locomotive operation, and for a fee, you too can spend time at the throttle. The museum's location along WP's Feather River Route makes it an ideal part of railway exploration of the famous canyon.

Orange Empire Railway Museum

For more than 50 years, the Orange Empire Railway Museum (OERM) has been a repository for historic railway equipment. Now one of the most extensive collections in the state, it covers a broad scope of California and western railway history. The museum is best known as the premier preservation site of Los Angeles–area electric railway equipment, restoring, exhibiting, and operating a variety of Pacific Electric and Los Angeles Railway streetcars and interurbans (more than a dozen PE Red Cars are onsite). The museum has also collected a wide array of traditional railroad cars and locomotives. Among the more significant cars in the collection is a former

Western Pacific Electro-Motive FP7A No. 805A is proudly displayed in its restored as-delivered scheme at the Feather River Rail Society's Western Pacific Railroad Museum in Portola, California. *Tom Kline*

If you're feeling nostalgic for Los Angeles electric railways, a visit to the Orange Empire Railway Museum can bring you back to the days when narrow gauge cars worked the streets. PCC car No. 3100—built in 1943—and L.A. Railways Type H-4 heavyweight No. 1201—built in 1921—work Broadway trackage at OERM, near Perris, California. *Brian Solomon*

In 1992, Santa Fe FP45 No. 98 leads an eastward intermodal train descending the east slope of the Tehachapis near Mojave, California. Today, this popular locomotive is preserved at the Orange Empire Railway Museum where its 20-cylinder 645E diesel can be heard working on selected weekends. *Brian Solomon*

Santa Fe Railway Post Office car. On the locomotive side, a former Ventura County Railway 2-6-2 Prairie-type is maintained in operable condition for occasional weekend service. To the delight of enthusiasts focused on more modern railroading, the museum operates a number of first- and second-generation diesels, including a former Southern Pacific U25B—General Electric's 2,500-horse-power road switcher that established the manufacturer as major player in the heavy-road diesel market in the early 1960s—and a Santa Fe FP45—a classic Electro-Motive Division 20-cylinder cowl model designed for Santa Fe passenger and freight services.

Since the mid-1990s, the OERM also has been the home for the Grizzly Flats collection of narrow gauge railroad equipment and artifacts. Assembled by the late Ward and Betty Kimball, this collection preserves an era

of 3-foot-gauge railroading that otherwise would have passed from memory. Ward was a well-known Disney animator who, in 1938, began collecting nineteenth-century narrow gauge railroad equipment and for many years displayed and operated the Grizzly Flats Railroad at his home in San Gabriel, California. Among the most significant item in this collection is a beautifully restored 2-6-0 Baldwin locomotive named *Emma Nevada*. Built in 1881, this locomotive typifies the moderately proportioned, well-adorned locomotives of the mid-Victorian era, of which only a few survive. The collection features maps and photographs describing the significant role of narrow gauge railroading in California with a number of interesting images of Southern Pacific's "Slim Princess" Carson & Colorado line that operated east of the Sierras.

The OERM is located on the site of an 1880s village called Pinacate, immediately south of modern-day Perris, California. Perris was named for the California Southern's chief engineer, Fred T. Perris, and the town was laid out on the Santa Fe's original line between San Diego, Colton, and San Bernardino. The museum operates a very short remnant section of the California Southern/Santa Fe line via Temecula Canyon for demonstration excursions. In addition, the museum has a 3-foot-6-inch-gauge streetcar loop for the operation of Los Angeles Railway cars.

The OERM's dry environment and dedicated membership has provided a safe haven for railway equipment, much of which would have been otherwise lost to scrappers. The OERM remains a work in progress, and while some equipment is operational, with a few pieces faithfully restored to original appearance, other equipment still awaits its day in the sun—or more accurately, its time in the shop. Much of the OERM's collection is protected by car barns and engine houses, and when these facilities are open to the public, visitors may explore the treasures within. Although much of the collection relates to California, there are a few choice curiosities as well, such as a Hill of Howth electric tram car from Dublin, Ireland.

San Pedro Red Cars

Hiding near the giant container cranes and deep-water berths of America's busiest port is one of Southern California's best-kept railway secrets: the Port of Los Angeles' historic Red Car Line in San Pedro. Since 2003, the Port of Los Angeles Pacific Harbor Line has hosted a short, public electric trolley car service. This line is part of a historic Pacific Electric route and remains an active freight route as well. When the tracks are not allocated for electric car services, they are part of the heavy-rail freight network that serves the port. Temporal separation ensures that when the Red Cars are on the move, there is no opportunity for an accidental interface with freight trains.

The Red Cars are more than just a historic demonstration. Some passengers opt for a roundtrip spin over the 1½-mile line, while others use the cars, which serve four regular stops near San Pedro's historic downtown area, as public transport. The Red Cars are also convenient for people who arrive by cruise ship and wish to tour the area.

At present, there are three electric cars: old No. 1058 was adapted from a vintage Pacific Electric wooden-bodied trolley built in 1913, while Nos. 500 and 501 are modern

Pacific Electric Red Car 501 makes for a pleasant contrast to the massive infrastructure necessary for the loading and unloading of international containers at the Port of Los Angeles. These cars offer one of the best ways to enjoy the port facility. *Brian Solomon*

replicas of wooden-bodied Pacific Electric cars built by the Port of Los Angeles and directly patterned after PE's vintage cars that operated on the line during the first three decades of the twentieth century. These cars feature all the detailing of the period, including varnished wood and brass fittings. On most days, the replica cars perform regular passenger services, with No. 1058 only venturing out for special occasions. The Red Cars operate at 20-minute intervals from 10 a.m. to 6 p.m., Friday to Monday. A passing siding near San Pedro's downtown station allows two cars to operate on the line at the same time.

While the Pacific Harbor Line tracks extend beyond the limits of present Red Car operation, the cars may not go beyond the limits of the overhead wires necessary to power them. The Port of Los Angeles has ambitious plans to extend Red Car operations both north and south of present limits.

CHAPTER 15

WESTERN RAILWAY MUSEUM

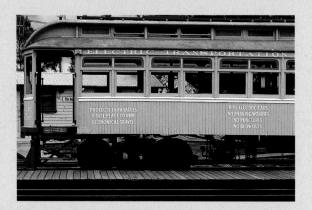

The Western Railway Museum (WRM) at Rio Vista Junction provides one of the finest preserved electric railway experiences in North America. It features an authentic 11-mile electric interurban train ride, short streetcar rides, and dozens of beautifully preserved railway cars and locomotives (protected in purpose-built car barns and shops). The museum is an outstanding tribute to its dedicated members and is well deserving of visits by railway enthusiasts and historians of all ages. In 2006, the museum attracted an estimated 25,000 visitors. In addition to weekend operations of electric trains, it offers a variety of attractions designed to appeal to families, casual visitors, and serious students of electric railways. The museum has been the ongoing project of the Bay Area Electric Railroad Association (BAERA), a group founded in 1946 with a desire to preserve the rapidly disappearing electric railway heritage of the Bay Area.

As electric railways faded from the scene in the 1940s and 1950s, the BAERA actively preserved examples of equipment, artifacts, and archives for future generations to appreciate and enjoy. In 1960, the

Facing page: The Western Railway Museum's articulated Key System bridge unit in the National City Lines livery operates against a backdrop of modern wind-turbine generators. *Brian Solomon*

Above: The Western Railway Museum at Rio Vista Junction has preserved a variety of the region's electric cars for public demonstration and excursions. This is a side view of interurban car No. 63. *Brian Solomon*

group established this museum at the historic Rio Vista Junction location along the old Sacramento Northern (SN) line. Situated in the Sacramento River delta's rolling grasslands, yet relatively close to population centers in the Bay Area, Sacramento, and Stockton, this location was recognized for its potential to re-create the atmosphere of an interurban electric railway while remaining free from congestion and complications of an urban environment. For more than three decades, the museum offered just a short streetcar loop, while the tracks of the adjacent Sacramento Northern line were still used by occasional local freights. The Western Railway Museum (officially named in 1985) acquired 22.5 miles of the adjacent former SN line from the Union Pacific in 1993. Trackage included a connection at Canon with the Southern Pacific (the UP since it acquired the SP in 1996) Cal-P route, a short branch from Canon to Dozier, and the former SN main line between Dozier, Rio Vista Junction, and Montezuma (near the old ferry terminal at Chips, California). Since that time, the WRM has refurbished and re-electrified more than 5

miles of the SN line for regular excursion use. Electric operations are limited by the effective reach of the museum's substation; a planned second substation would enable extension of wire.

Improvements to the Western Railway Museum have included the 2001 opening of the large, climate-controlled visitor's center and archive, built in Mission revival style resembling regional railway stations. It houses the museum's store, a variety of displays relating to area electric lines (including scale models of SN's Suisun Straits ferries), a small canteen serving snacks and beverages, and the museum's extensive library. Ample parking and access from California Highway 12 make it easy to reach the museum by car (unfortunately, at present there is no practical means to arrive by rail).

In May 2008, the museum dedicated its Loring C. Jensen Memorial Car House, a $2.2 million investment and a major step forward in the preservation of its railway equipment. This 38,000-square-foot structure covers six tracks and allows for safer storage of railway equipment

Peninsular Railway No. 52 poses atop a wooden-pile trestle along the Western Railway Museum's former Sacramento Northern interurban electric line. No. 52 is a regular runner at the WRM. The car was built by the St. Louis Car Company for the San Jose & Los Gatos Interurban Railway. *Brian Solomon*

while providing a more effective public display of the museum's collection. It is the most expensive project undertaken thus far by the museum.

Among the WRM's operating equipment are several beautifully restored examples of early-twentieth-century interurban electrics that once served towns and cities in the Bay Area. Peninsular Railway No. 52 is a classic wooden-bodied interurban car, typical of those that worked lines on the southern San Francisco Peninsula connecting San Jose with Palo Alto, Cupertino, and Los Gatos. At the other end of the interurban spectrum are several former Key System bridge units (see sidebar) built in the late 1930s using aluminum articulated bodies. Where Peninsular Railway 52 looks like something that rolled out of the Victorian age, the articulated bridge units seem relatively modern, although their design is now nearly 70 years old. Many younger visitors to the museum are surprised to learn that Key System trains such as these regularly whisked passengers across the lower deck of the Bay Bridge.

Above left: The Western Railway Museum offers weekend excursions over its electrified former Sacramento Northern line. The car's operator adjusts the trolley pole to the wire for the return trip to Rio Vista Junction. *Brian Solomon*

Above right: An interior view of a Key System bridge unit at the Western Railway Museum. As late as 1958, these aluminum-bodied cars whisked passengers between San Francisco and the East Bay over the lower deck of the Bay Bridge. *Brian Solomon*

BAY AREA ELECTRIC RAILWAYS

Along with its interurban trains, the Sacramento Northern provided local transit services to some communities along its lines. A Western Pacific freight led by Baldwin-built Mikado 309 pauses at the Marysville Station alongside an SN Birney car in local service. The SN's passenger trolleys concluded regular service at Marysville in 1949, while WP was completely dieselized in 1953. *Bay Area Electric Railroad Association at the Western Railroad Museum Archive*

In the first decades of the twentieth century, electric railways, including both street railways and interurban electric lines, played a crucial role in Bay Area development. The region hosted different electric railway schemes and was thus blessed with some of the best electric railway services in the West. All railways, except the San Francisco Muni, were conceived with private capital as money-making ventures. In the North Bay, Northwestern Pacific provided an intensive third-rail service from various cities in Marin County to the ferry pier at Sausalito. San Francisco was served by Muni and the Market Street Railway. The East Bay was connected with lines of the Key System, Southern Pacific's East Bay electric lines, and the Oakland, Antioch & Eastern (OA&E and, later Sacramento Northern).

The OA&E/SN line is of special interest to visitors to the Western Railway Museum. In its heyday, the OA&E route was part of a 93-mile line between Sacramento and San Francisco that became part of Western Pacific's Sacramento Northern interurban empire in 1928. This line hosted nine roundtrip passenger services daily and served as a freight feeder for WP. One of the quirks of this operation was its rail ferry service. Since SN didn't have a bridge over the Suisun Straits of the Sacramento River delta, it used specially equipped rail ferries for a through service. Regular passenger service ended in 1940, and wires were removed in 1953 when the ferry was abandoned and through freight services ended (portions of the SN line survived for nominal local freight traffic). In 1982, Union Pacific acquired SN's parent, Western Pacific. By the 1990s, although portions of the old

SN line remained, many tracks were largely disused. The Western Railway Museum acquired one of these SN segments.

The influence of electric railways on the Bay Area was significant but relatively short lived. Improvements to public highways and increased private automobile ownership had disastrous effects on electric railway ridership. Another change was the construction of the trans-bay bridges. Passengers traveling to San Francisco by rail had traditionally taken ferries across the bay. The opening of the Golden Gate Bridge in 1937 and the San Francisco–Oakland Bay Bridge in 1938 effectively ended the classic era of trans-bay ferries, while further devastating electric railway passenger traffic. Although both bridges were conceived with the capacity to carry electric railway lines, only the Bay Bridge was built with tracks (on its lower deck). As noted, SN's services ended in 1940 and electric passenger services on NWP and SP East Bay electric lines ended in 1941. The Key System picked up some of SP's routes and continued to provide service over the Bay Bridge using modern aluminum-bodied articulated cars known as bridge units. After World War II, Key System was acquired by National City Lines, known for its highway transport connections and biases (it was controlled by a consortium including General Motors). Under NCL, rail operations were rapidly scaled back and replaced with buses. The Key System's final rail operations were its Bay Bridge services that were discontinued in 1958. Two years later, remaining Key System bus routes were conveyed to East Bay bus operator AC Transit (Alameda and Contra Costa counties).

Among the variety of streetcars from San Francisco and the East Bay is Muni 1001, the last surviving so-called "Magic Carpet," a type famous for its smooth-riding qualities. This double-ended streamlined car closely resembles the PCCs in service on Muni's historic F Line in San Francisco, but with several technical differences. No. 1001 was bought by Muni before World War II and does not employ the patented electric gear and desktop-style controls normally used by true PCCs. In 2008, the WRM also had a single-ended Muni PCC undergoing a thorough restoration. When complete, this car is expected to see occasional service on the WRM's streetcar loop. Other streetcars include Key System No. 352, built in 1911 and restored to the livery used by the street railway in 1931. One of the nicest cars and among the most

fun to ride—though not the smoothest—is Sacramento Northern No. 62, a four-wheel Birney car (named for its designer, Charles O. Birney). An early one-man car type (referring to its operation), the Birney car was popular with street railways for lightly traveled lines. Cars like the Birney were the last to regularly work SN's final passenger runs in Sacramento, Marysville, and Chico local services after World War II.

Streetcars use the same essential technology as interurban electrics but tend to be lower and lighter, designed for slower-speed street running. As a general rule, streetcar wheels also have smaller flanges. As a result, the museum's streetcars are only operated on the trolley loop and do not venture out onto the WRM's former Sacramento Northern interurban line.

The Western Railway Museum at Rio Vista Junction gives visitors the opportunity to experience a variety of period electric cars. Former Sacramento Northern Birney safety car No. 62 and Muni "Magic Carpet" car No. 1003 are among the museum's operational streetcars. *Brian Solomon*

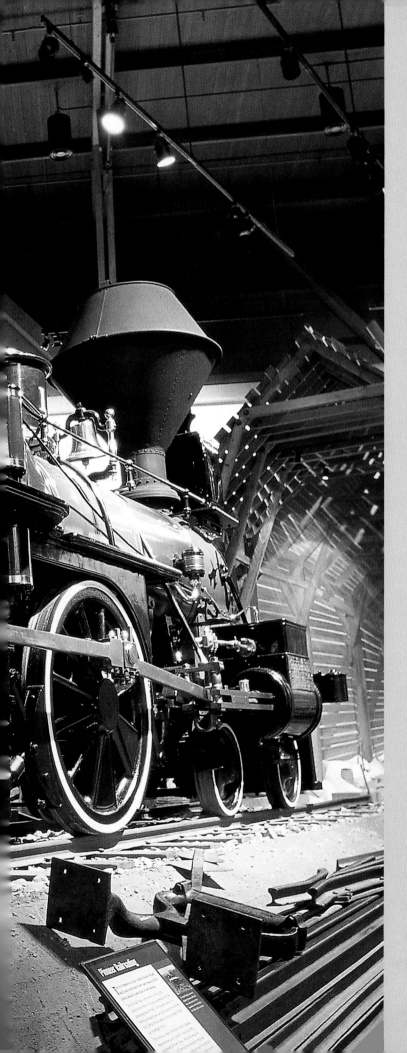

CHAPTER 16

CALIFORNIA STATE RAILROAD MUSEUM AND THE SIERRA RAILWAY

Two of California's finest examples of railway preservation are operated by the California State Railroad Museum: one is the state's most significant collection of historic railway equipment, displayed in modern buildings specifically constructed for the purpose near Old Town Sacramento, and extensive archives housed nearby; the other is an authentic, operating excursion railway based at period-built facilities in the Sierra foothills at Jamestown. Combined, they represent one of the most significant railway preservation efforts in North America.

California State Railroad Museum
Nothing in California compares with the scope or presentation of the California State Railroad Museum (CSRM), the state's premier railroad preservation venue and Sacramento's largest tourist attraction. Strategically situated a few blocks east of the state capitol building, adjacent to Old Town

Facing page: Central Pacific's first locomotive was *Governor Stanford*, a classic 4-4-0 that first steamed at Sacramento on September 10, 1863. It is featured in the CSRM's Donner Pass display that conveys the size of the original wooden snow sheds. Owing to exceptional Sierra snow, CP began experimenting with snow sheds in 1867. Ultimately more than 30 miles of shed covered the line. *Brian Solomon*

Above: The Sierra Railroad's Joe Bispo observes the crew of locomotive No. 28 at Jamestown. This popular little railroad is kept alive by a dedicated staff. *Brian Solomon*

Above left: The California State Railroad Museum displays North Pacific Coast No. 12, a 3-foot gauge 4-4-0 with two narrow gauge coaches. Built by Baldwin in 1876, this locomotive first served the North Pacific Coast, a narrow gauge railway built in the 1870s and 1880s between Sausalito and the Russian River. In later years, the NPC became part of the Northwestern Pacific, although by that time this locomotive had found work on the Nevada Central, where it operated until the 1930s. *Brian Solomon*

Above right: Visitors flock to the California State Railroad Museum for Railfair '99. In addition to the CSRM's regular displays, celebrity locomotives—including Southern Pacific GS-4 No. 4449, Sierra Railway No. 28, and Thomas the Tank Engine—thrilled the next generation of railroad enthusiasts. *Tom Kline*

Sacramento and near the railroad station, its location is central to California's early railroad history and part of the museum's attraction. Sacramento was home to California's earliest successful railroad, along with the beginnings of the first Transcontinental Railroad and its original western terminal and primary shops. Because California owes its rapid development to its railroads, the CSRM is a fitting tribute to the state's history.

Located on the site of Central Pacific's original terminal, the CSRM features historic buildings, including the famous Huntington & Hopkins Hardware Store where CP got its formative start. Across the tracks is the site of the Central Pacific (later Southern Pacific) shop complex where locomotives were manufactured and maintained for more than 100 years. In its day, Central Pacific was remarkably self-sufficient—these shops were the location of considerable innovation in the formative days of California railroading.

In 1976, a re-creation of Central Pacific's original Sacramento terminus was opened to the public. This event was a prelude to the opening of impressive modern facilities in 1981, an event that coincided with the first Sacramento Railfair—a grand celebration that saw historic locomotives and equipment converge on Sacramento from around the nation.

Its history and buildings provide the backdrop to the CSRM's main attraction: the West's most significant and best preserved collection of railroad equipment. Visitors to the CSRM are awed by its magnificent equipment displays.

Its centerpiece is the Southern Pacific AC-12 No. 4294, the last built and only surviving example of SP's famous cab-forward articulated steam locomotives. Proudly displayed in the museum's main hall, this massive machine dwarfs everything around it. In its day, the cab-forward was SP's standard road locomotive assigned to Donner Pass and other SP mountain crossings. SP developed the cab-forward concept before World War I for operations in the confines of Donner's snow sheds and tunnels. With the cab in front of the boiler, crews were afforded better forward visibility and were less affected by the exhaust gases that plagued conventional locomotives. The AC-12 represents the final phase of development for this unusual type of steam locomotive.

Putting the enormous size of the cab-forward in perspective is the perfectly proportioned and pint-sized 4-4-0 American-type *Sonoma*, engine No. 12. Built by Baldwin in 1876 for the narrow gauge North Pacific Coast, old No. 12 is a classic wood-burner featuring the adornment and style associated with a mid-Victorian period locomotive. Although it served in California for only a few years, this engine spent most of its operating life on the Nevada Central Railway. By the end of its career in the 1930s, it was recognized as an antique gem and set aside for preservation by the railway's manager, J. M. Hiskey. Behind it are two well-preserved period passenger cars, typical of those used on western branch lines in the mid-nineteenth century.

The crucial role of Donner Pass and its difficult construction is conveyed in a diorama featuring a re-created snow shed and Central Pacific's first locomotive, the famed

Southern Pacific cab-ahead No. 4294 and the Virginia & Truckee *Empire* are finely displayed at the California State Railroad Museum. Built by Baldwin in 1944, No. 4294 had a short service life, working for only about a dozen years before it was replaced by diesels during the 1950s. It has spent more than twice as much time displayed at the CSRM as it did working trains on SP. *Brian Solomon*

Governor Stanford, named for influential businessman and politician Leland Stanford, one of the Big Four that built the CP and SP empires.

Also among the many steam locomotives displayed is a Western Pacific F7A diesel-electric. Electro-Motive's streamlined F-unit models displaced steam from freight service in the late 1940s and early 1950s. This WP engine was one of the last four F-units in regular freight service in California and long popular with railway enthusiasts.

The CSRM's locomotives draw people to the museum, but these units represent just a portion of the museum's displays and the railroad's story. A good variety of railroad cars are also displayed and interpreted. For example, the Fruit Growers Express refrigerated boxcar was one of tens

of thousands of "reefers" that once graced western rails, operating in solid trains known as "fruit blocks" that delivered California produce eastward. In the days before mechanical refrigeration, heavily insulated reefers, such as the one on display at the CSRM, were filled with large blocks of salted ice to keep produce at desired temperatures.

Among the most significant passenger cars displayed is the Santa Fe dining car *Cochiti,* built by Budd in 1937 for the original *Super Chief* streamlined consist. This diner was among the earliest of the Budd-built streamlined cars that defined American long-distance rail travel for more than two decades. The car represents the high quality of service once offered by private railroads across the United States. Visitors may walk through the car and imagine dining with movie stars against the rolling backdrop of the Southwest.

Presentation is crucial to the CSRM's displays. The museum has gone to great lengths not just to preserve, restore, and exhibit significant railroad equipment, but to interpret and explain the significance of each piece. Succinct descriptions that relay important details are accompanied by relevant historic photographs and artifacts. In addition to rolling stock, the CSRM reveals the role of various railroad crafts. Its displays describe the often-overlooked jobs, such as that of section gangs (local maintenance forces), as well as the women railroaders employed in large numbers during World War II. In addition to the finely preserved machines on display, the CSRM has gathered a substantial collection of historic equipment stored out of public view and awaiting restoration.

Most of the CSRM's exhibits are static displays, but the museum also provides a demonstration excursion using former Southern Pacific heavyweight cars over a 3-mile section of SP's Walnut Grove branch. This line runs compass south (SP treated its entire system as an east–west operation) along the Sacramento River. The branch itself was built to serve agriculture in the Sacramento River delta, and portions of the line still see regular freight service provided by the CSRM with interchange from Union Pacific.

The CSRM also maintains an extensive archive of books and historical documents. This archive is normally open to researchers on weekday afternoons. Tens of thousands of documents, including vintage timetables, railroad records, photographs, and maps are housed there. It could take several lifetimes to digest the scope of the archives, but even a few hours in the library will give a visitor a greater appreciation of the equipment and artifacts preserved for display.

Above: Dressed in period attire at Jamestown, Sierra Railway car host Darryl Bramlette stands in front of parlor observation car No. 2901. Built in 1910, this deluxe open-end Pullman observation car gives the Sierra's first-class passengers a taste of the golden age of railroad passenger travel. *Brian Solomon*

Right: Sierra Railway locomotive No. 28 can be seen in the mirror at the center of former SP open-end observation car No. 2901. *Brian Solomon*

Sierra Railway

A visit to the Sierra Railway at Jamestown may produce a sense of déjà vu, even if you have never traveled there before. The reason for its familiarity is simple: over the last 90 years, the Sierra Railway has been featured in dozens of Hollywood films and television programs. Although its Jamestown facilities owe their longevity, in part, to movie productions, this railroad is no Hollywood set. The railroad's roundhouse, shops, cars, and locomotives are authentic and together provide a rare look at the California branch-line railroading once common and now all but extinct. The Sierra retains all the charm and character of early-twentieth-century western railroading for modern visitors to enjoy.

The Sierra Railway got its start in 1897 when William H. Crocker (son of the late Charles Crocker of the Big Four) and two partners founded the line. They were attracted by the prospects of moving lucrative mining traffic from the foothills to market. Ground was broken at a connection with Southern Pacific at Oakdale in March of that year. By November, track crews had completed 41 miles of line to the Sierra foothills village of Jamestown, 1,475 feet above sea level. The railroad's first passenger train arrived in Jamestown on November 8, 1897. In the beginning, the railroad served mining interests, and Jamestown rapidly developed into a boomtown with all the associated flair and Old West characters.

Mining traffic was only part of the Sierra's story. The railroad's promoters had grand visions of pushing the line over Sonoma Pass and possibly evolving as a transcontinental link. By 1900, the Sierra's main line reached Tuolumne City, 57 miles from its connection with Southern Pacific. While the Sierra Railway never conquered its namesake mountain range and transcontinental ambitions were fulfilled by other lines, the railroad instead developed as a trunk for a host of mountain lines in the region. A branch from Jamestown was extended up an exceptionally steep grade to Angels Camp. Within a few years, lumber traffic was augmenting the Sierra Railway's mining traffic. A number of winding narrow gauge railways, including the famed West Side Lumber Company and Pickering Lumber, fed timber business to the Sierra. These sinuous lines using steep grades and switchbacks tapped timber stands in the canyons and mountainsides of the Sierras where no standard gauge railroad would ever reach. In the 1920s and 1930s, more connecting lines were built in conjunction with dam construction, such as the famous Hetch Hetchy dam, designed to trap Sierra snowmelt for both water and electricity.

The Great Depression forced reorganization and resulted in a name change to the Sierra Railroad. After World War II, the line flourished again, although its branches and feeders gradually were abandoned. In 1955, the Sierra replaced steam in regular service with a small fleet of Baldwin diesels to haul its freight trains. Yet steam never really died. As a result of continued Hollywood interest, the railroad retained its steam locomotives and repair shops. By 1970, the company acknowledged the

Jamestown's Sierra Railway is one of the state's treasures and home to one of the last traditional roundhouses in the western United States. On a warm morning, Sierra Railway No. 28 comes up to pressure inside the roundhouse before its busy day hauling excursions. Years ago, this locomotive was kept busy moving freight. *Brian Solomon*

nostalgic value of its Jamestown shops by opening them to the public as the aptly named museum, Railtown 1897. Changes in the railroad's business resulted in the separation of its historic operations from the freight operations in the early 1980s. The Jamestown shop facilities and vintage equipment were largely conveyed to the State of California. Since 1992, the Railtown 1897 park and train ride have been managed by the California State Railroad Museum. Today, the historic Sierra Railway operates seasonal weekend steam and diesel excursions using trackage rights on 3 miles of the Sierra Railroad, the latter now being a privately operated common-carrier short line that still operates freight services and seasonal, diesel-hauled, dinner train excursions.

For visitors and railway enthusiasts, the Sierra Railway's big draw is its period atmosphere and historic authenticity. Old No. 28, a handsome 2-8-0, was built new by Baldwin for the Sierra Railway back in 1922. This locomotive is the real thing; neither a replica nor a locomotive bought by a Johnny-come-lately tourist railway and dressed up strictly for entertainment. When No. 28 eases out of the roundhouse under stream and is turned on the turntable, it's doing so on home rails.

The roundhouse itself is one of Railtown 1897's greatest attributes. Once common in railroad towns across North America, roundhouses became largely unnecessary with conversions to diesel. Very few have survived, and they are especially rare in the West. The Sierra's roundhouse was built about 1910, after the railroad's original four-stall structure was destroyed by fire. The Sierra Railway also maintains one of the last belt-driven shops in the country (in the early days of mechanized machine shops, a single large prime mover—originally steam—would drive numerous distributed devices via a series of interconnected leather belts. This technique was made obsolete by the invention of the small electric motor in the 1900s).

The railroad cars on the property largely date from the 1910 to 1920 period. Dearly loved by railroad enthusiasts, modelers, and filmmakers alike are shorty passenger coach No. 6 and combine No. 5, built for service on the Angels Camp branches' exceptionally tight curvature. These units are only taken out for special events but may be viewed in the stalls of the roundhouse.

A day out on the Sierra is more than just a railway excursion in the foothills—it is a step back to a time when branch-line railroading was king of the mountain.

BIBLIOGRAPHY

BOOKS, REPORTS, AND MONOGRAPHS

Allen, G. Freeman. *The Fastest Trains in the World.* London: Ian Allan, 1978.

Anderson, Craig T. *Amtrak: The National Railroad Passenger Corporation 1978–1979 Annual.* San Francisco: Rail Transportation Archives, 1978.

Armstrong, John H. *The Railroad: What It Is, What It Does.* Omaha, Neb.: Simmons-Boardman, 1982.

Asay, Jeff S. *Track and Time: An Operational History of the Western Pacific Railroad through Timetables and Maps.* Portola, Calif.: Feather River Rail Society, 2006.

Austin, Ed, and Tom Dill. *The Southern Pacific in Oregon.* Edmonds, Wash.: Pacific Fast Mail, 1987.

Bancroft, Hubert Howe, Henry L. Oak, William Nemos, and Frances F. Victor. *History of California, Vol. VII.* San Francisco: The History Company, 1890.

Beebe, Lucius. *The Central Pacific and the Southern Pacific Railroads.* Berkeley, Calif.: Howell-North, 1963.

—. *The Overland Limited.* Berkeley, Calif.: Howell-North, 1963.

Benson, Ted. *Mother Lode Shortline: A Sierra Railroad Pictorial.* Burlingame, Calif.: Chatham, 1970.

Best, Gerald M. *Snowplow: Clearing Mountain Rails.* Berkeley, Calif.: Howell-North, 1966.

Borden, Stanley T. *History and Rosters of the Northwestern Pacific Railroad and Predecessor Lines.* San Mateo, Calif.: Western Railroader, 1949.

Bradley, Rodger. *Amtrak: The US National Railroad Passenger Corporation.* Dorset, U.K.: Blandford, 1985.

Bruce, Alfred W. *The Steam Locomotive in America: Its Development in the Twentieth Century.* New York: Norton, 1952.

Bush, Donald J. *The Streamlined Decade.* New York: Braziller, 1975.

Churella, Albert, J. *From Steam to Diesel: Managerial Customs and Organizational Capabilities in the Twentieth-Century American Locomotive Industry.* Princeton, N.J.: Princeton University Press, 1998.

Conomos, T. J., ed. *San Francisco Bay: The Urbanized Estuary.* San Francisco: Pacific Division of AAAS, 1979.

Cook, Richard J. *Super Power Steam Locomotives.* San Marino, Calif.: Golden West, 1966.

Crump, Spencer. *The Skunk Railroad: Fort Bragg to Willits.* Los Angeles: Trans-Anglo Books, 1964.

Daggett, Stuart. *Chapters on the History of the Southern Pacific.* New York: Ronald Press, 1922.

Darton, N. H. *Guidebook of the Western United States: Part C. The Santa Fe Route with a Side Trip to the Grand Canyon of the Colorado.* Washington, D.C.: Government Printing Office, 1915.

Deane, Dorothy Newell. *Sierra Railway.* Berkeley, Calif.: Howell-North, 1960.

Demorro, Harry W. *The Key Route Part I.* Glendale, Calif.: Interurban Press, 1985.

DeNevi, Don. *The Western Pacific: Railroading Yesterday, Today and Tomorrow.* Seattle: Superior Publishing, 1978.

Dethier, Jean. *Le Temps des Gares.* Paris: Centre Georges Pompidou, 1978. Republished as *All Stations: A Journey through 150 Years of Railway History.* London: Thames and Hudson, 1981.

Diller, J. S., and others. *Guidebook of the Western United States: Part D. The Shasta Route and Coast Line.* Washington, D.C.: Government Printing Office, 1916.

Droege, John A. *Passenger Terminals and Trains.* New York: McGraw-Hill, 1916.

Dubin, Arthur D. *Some Classic Trains.* Milwaukee, Wis.: Kalmbach, 1964.

—. *More Classic Trains.* Milwaukee, Wis.: Kalmbach, 1974.

Duke, Donald. *Southern Pacific Steam Locomotives: A Pictorial Anthology of Western Railroading.* San Marino, Calif.: Pacific Railway Journal, 1962.

—. *Union Pacific in Southern California 1890–1990.* San Marino, Calif.: Golden West, 2005.

Duke, Donald, and Stan Kistler. *Santa Fe: Steel Rails through California.* San Marino, Calif.: Golden West, 1963.

Dunscomb, Guy, L. *A Century of Southern Pacific Steam Locomotives, 1862–1962.* Modesto, Calif.: Dunscomb, 1963.

Farrington, Jr., S. Kip. *Railroads at War.* New York: Coward-McCann, 1944.

—. *Railroading from the Rear End.* New York: Coward-McCann, 1946.

—. *Railroads of Today.* New York: Coward-McCann, 1949.

—. *Railroading the Modern Way.* New York: Coward-McCann, 1951.

—. *Railroads of the Hour.* New York: Coward-McCann, 1958.

Frailey, Fred W. *Zephyrs, Chiefs & Other Orphans: The First Five Years of Amtrak.* Godfrey, Ill.: RPC Publications, 1977.

—. *Twilight of the Great Trains.* Waukesha, Wis.: Kalmbach, 1998.

Garmany, John B. *Southern Pacific Dieselization.* Edmonds, Wash.: Pacific Fast Mail, 1985.

Harlan, George H. *San Francisco Bay Ferryboats.* Berkeley, Calif.: Howell-North, 1967.

Hanscom, W. W., and Walt Wheelock. *The Archaeology of the Cable Car.* Pasadena, Calif.: Socio-Technical Books, 1970.

Heath, Erle. *Seventy-Five Years of Progress: Historical Sketch of the Southern Pacific.* San Francisco: Southern Pacific Bureau of News, 1945.

Hedges, James Blaine. *Henry Villard and the Railways of the Northwest.* New York: H. Milford, Oxford University Press, 1930.

Hidy, Ralph W., Muriel E. Hidy, Roy V. Scott, and Don L. Hofsommer. *The Great Northern Railway.* Boston: Harvard Business School Press, 1988.

Hilton, George W. *The Cable Car in America: A New Treatise upon Cable or Rope Traction as Applied to the Working of Street and Other Railways.* San Diego: Howell-North, 1982.

—. *American Narrow Gauge Railroads.* Palo Alto, Calif.: Stanford University Press, 1990.

Hofsommer, Donovan L. *The Southern Pacific, 1901–1985.* College Station, Texas: Texas A&M University Press, 1986.

Hollander, Stanley, C. *Passenger Transportation: Readings Selected from a Marketing Viewpoint.* Lansing, Mich.: Bureau of Business and Economic Research, Michigan State University, 1968.

Jenkins, Arthur C. *A Report on Economic and Organizational Features of the Municipal Railway of San Francisco to the Honorable Board of Supervisors, City and County of San Francisco.* San Francisco: Arthur C. Jenkins, 1949.

Jennison, Brian, and Victor Neves. *Southern Pacific Oregon Division.* Mukilteo, Wash.: Hundman Publishing, 1997.

Keilty, Edmund. *Interurbans without Wires: The Rail Motorcar in the United States.* Glendale, Calif.: Interurbans, 1979.

Kirkland, John F. *Dawn of the Diesel Age: The History of the Diesel Locomotive in America.* Pasadena, Calif.: Interurban Press, 1983.

—. *The Diesel Builders, Vol. 1: Fairbanks-Morse and Lima-Hamilton.* Glendale, Calif.: Interurban Press, 1985.

—. *The Diesel Builders, Vol. 2: American Locomotive Company and Montreal Locomotive Works.* Glendale, Calif.: Interurban Press, 1989.

—. *The Diesel Builders, Vol. 3: Baldwin Locomotive Works.* Glendale, Calif.: Interurban Press, 1994.

Klein, Maury. *The Life & Legend of E. H. Harriman.* Chapel Hill, N.C.: University of North Carolina Press, 2000.

—. *Union Pacific: Vol. 1, 1862–1893.* Minneapolis: University of Minnesota Press, 2006.

Lewis, Oscar. *The Big Four: The Story of Huntington, Stanford, Hopkins, and Crocker, and of the Building of the Central Pacific.* New York: A. A. Knopf, 1938.

Marre, Louis A. *Diesel Locomotives: The First 50 Years: A Guide to Diesels Built Before 1972.* Waukesha, Wis.: Kalmbach, 1995.

Marre, Louis A., and Paul K. Withers. *The Contemporary Diesel Spotter's Guide: A Comprehensive Reference Manual to Locomotives Since 1972.* Halifax, Pa.: Withers Publishing, 2000.

Marshall, James L. *Santa Fe: The Railroad That Built an Empire.* New York: Random House, 1945.

McKane, John, and Anthony Perles. *Inside Muni: The Properties and Operations of the Municipal Railway of San Francisco.* Glendale, Calif.: Interurban Press, 1982.

McMillan, Joe. *Santa Fe's Diesel Fleet.* Burlingame, Calif.: Chatham Publishing, 1975.

Middleton, William D. *When the Steam Railroads Electrified.* Milwaukee, Wis.: Kalmbach, 1974.

—. *From Bullets to BART: Bulletin No. 127.* Chicago: Central Electric Railfans' Association, 1989.

Myrick, David F. *Life and Times of the Central Pacific Railroad.* San Francisco: Book Club of California, 1969.

—. *Western Pacific: The Last Transcontinental Railroad* (Colorado Rail Annual, No. 27). Golden, Colo.: Colorado Railroad Museum, 2006.

Palmer, Phil, and Mike Palmer. *The Cable Cars of San Francisco.* Berkeley, Calif.: Howell-North, 1959.

Perini, Jimo. *San Francisco Grip.* San Francisco: San Francisco Grip Publishers, 1969.

Perles, Anthony. *The People's Railway: The History of the Municipal Railway of San Francisco.* Glendale, Calif.: Interurban Press, 1981.

—. *Tours of Discovery: A San Francisco Muni Album.* Glendale, Calif.: Interurban Press, 1984.

Pinkepank, Jerry A. *The Second Diesel Spotter's Guide.* Milwaukee, Wis.: Kalmbach, 1973.

Pope, Dan, and Mark Lynn. *Warbonnets: From Super Chief to Super Fleet.* Waukesha, Wis.: Pentrex Media Group, 1994.

Potter, Janet Greenstein. *Great American Railroad Stations.* New York: Preservation Press, 1996.

Riegel, Robert Edgar. *The Story of the Western Railroads: From 1852 through the Reign of the Giants.* Lincoln, Neb.: University of Nebraska Press, 1926.

Ryan, Dennis, and Joseph W. Shine. *Southern Pacific Passenger Trains.* La Mirada, Calif.: Four Ways West Publications, 1986.

—. *Southern Pacific Passenger Trains, Vol. 2.* La Mirada, Calif.: Four Ways West Publications, 2000.

Ryczkowski, John J., Dan Crews, and Pete Miller. *Western Pacific Pictorial.* Sparks, Nev.: Steel Rails West Publishing, 1979.

Sabin, Edwin, L. *Building the Pacific Railway: The Construction Story of America's First Iron Thoroughfare Between the Missouri River and California.* Philadelphia: J. B. Lippincott, 1919.

Sappers, Vernon J. *Key System Streetcars: Transit, Real Estate, and the Growth of the East Bay.* Wilton, Calif.: Signature Press, 2007.

Saunders, Richard. *The Railroad Mergers and the Coming of Conrail.* Westport, Conn.: Greenwood Press, 1978.

—. *Merging Lines: American Railroads, 1900–1970.* DeKalb, Ill.: Northern Illinois University Press, 2001.

—. *Main Lines: Rebirth of the North American Railroads, 1970–2002.* DeKalb, Ill.: Northern Illinois University Press, 2003.

Schafer, Mike. *All Aboard Amtrak.* Piscataway, N.J.: Railpace Co., 1991.

Shearer, Frederick. E. *The Pacific Tourist: Adams & Bishop's Illustrated Trans-continental Guide of Travel, from the Atlantic to the Pacific Ocean.* New York: Bounty Books, 1970.

Signor, John R. *Rails in the Shadow of Mt. Shasta: 100 Years of Railroading along Southern Pacific's Shasta Division.* San Diego: Howell-North, 1982.

—. *Tehachapi.* San Marino, Calif.: Golden West Books, 1983.

—. *Donner Pass: Southern Pacific's Sierra Crossing.* San Marino, Calif.: Golden West Books, 1985.

—. *Beaumont Hill: Southern Pacific's Southern California Gateway.* San Marino, Calif.: Golden West Books, 1990.

—. *Southern Pacific's Coast Line.* Wilton, Calif.: Signature Press, 1994.

—. *Southern Pacific's Western Division.* Wilton, Calif.: Signature Press, 2003.

Simburger, Edward J. *A Complete Guide to the Los Angeles Metrolink Commuter Train System: Covering Los Angeles, Orange, Riverside, San Bernardino, and Ventura Counties.* Agoura, Calif.: Yerba Seca Publications, 1996.

Sinclair, Angus. *Development of the Locomotive Engine.* New York: D. Van Nostrand, 1907.

Snyder, Dave. *The Path to a Livable City.* San Francisco, 2002.

Solomon, Brian. *Trains of the Old West.* New York: MetroBooks, 1998.

—. *American Steam Locomotive.* Osceola, Wis.: Motorbooks International, 1998.

—. *Southern Pacific Railroad.* Osceola, Wis.: Motorbooks International, 1999.

—. *The American Diesel Locomotive.* Osceola, Wis.: MBI Publishing Company, 2000.

—. *Super Steam Locomotives.* Osceola, Wis.: MBI Publishing Company, 2000.

—. *Locomotive.* Osceola, Wis.: MBI Publishing Company, 2001.

—. *Railroad Signaling.* St. Paul, Minn.: MBI Publishing Company, 2003.

——. *Santa Fe Railway*. St. Paul, Minn.: MBI Publishing Company, 2003.

——. *Amtrak*. St. Paul, Minn.: MBI Publishing Company, 2004.

——. *Burlington Northern Santa Fe Railway*. St. Paul, Minn.: MBI Publishing Company, 2005.

——. *Southern Pacific Passenger Trains*. St. Paul, Minn.: MBI Publishing Company, 2005.

Staff, Virgil. *D-Day on the Western Pacific: A Railroad's Decision to Dieselize*. Glendale, Calif.: Interurban Press, 1982.

Stegmaier, Harry. *Southern Pacific Passenger Train Consists and Cars 1955-1958*. Lynchburg, Va.: TLC Publishing, 2001.

Stindt, Fred A. *The Northwestern Pacific Railroad: Redwood Empire Route*. Redwood City, Calif.: Fred A. Stindt, 1964.

——. *San Francisco's Century of Street Cars*. Kelseyville, Calif.: Stindt Books, 1990.

Strapac, Joseph A. *Southern Pacific Motive Power Annuals*. Burlingame, Calif., 1968–1972.

——. *Southern Pacific Review 1981*. Huntington Beach, Calif.: Pacific Coast Chapter of the Railway and Locomotive Historical Society, 1982.

——. *Southern Pacific Review, 1952–82*. Huntington Beach, Calif.: Railway & Locomotive Historical Society, 1983.

——. *Southern Pacific Review 1953–1985*. Huntington Beach, Calif.: Railway & Locomotive Historical Society, 1986.

——. *Southern Pacific Historic Diesels Vols. 3–10*. Huntington Beach, Calif., and Bellflower, Calif.: Railway & Locomotive Historical Society, 2003.

Tahja, Katy M. *Rails across the Noyo: A Rider's Guide to the Skunk Train*. Comptche, 2008.

Thoms, William E. *Reprieve for the Iron Horse: The Amtrak Experiment, Its Predecessors and Prospects*. Baton Rouge, La.: Claitor's Publishing Division, 1973.

Thompson, Gregory Lee. *The Passenger Train in the Motor Age: California's Rail and Bus Industries, 1910–1941*. Columbus, Ohio: Ohio State University Press, 1993.

U.S. Senate. Joint Special Committee to Investigate Chinese Immigration. *Report of the Joint Special Committee to Investigate Chinese Immigration*. Washington: Government Printing Office, 1877.Waters, L. L. *Steel Trails to Santa Fe*. Lawrence, Kan.: University of Kansas Press, 1950.

Wilson, Neill C., and Frank J. Taylor. *Southern Pacific: The Roaring Story of a Fighting Railroad*. New York: McGraw-Hill, 1952.

Wright, Richard K. *Southern Pacific Daylight*. Thousand Oaks, Calif.: Wright Enterprises, 1970.

——. *America's Bicentennial Queen, Engine 4449: "The Lone Survivor."* Oakhurst, Calif.: Wright Enterprises, 1975.

PERIODICALS

CTC Board: Railroads Illustrated. Ferndale, Wash.

Diesel Era Magazine. Halifax, Pa.

Diesel Railway Traction (supplement to *Railway Gazette*, U.K.). [Merged into *Railway Gazette*.]

Jane's World Railways. London.

Locomotive & Railway Preservation. Waukesha, Wis. [no longer published]

Official Guide to the Railways. New York. [no longer published]

Passenger Train Journal. Waukesha, Wis.

Passenger Train Annual, Nos. 3 & 4. Park Forest, Ill. [no longer published]

RailNews. Waukesha, Wis. [no longer published]

Railway Age. Chicago and New York.

Railway Signaling and Communications (formerly *The Railway Signal Engineer*, neé, *Railway Signaling*). Chicago and New York.

Railway Gazette, The. London.

Railroad History (formerly *Railway and Locomotive Historical Society Bulletin*). Boston.

San Francisco Chronicle. San Francisco.

San Francisco Examiner. San Francisco.

Southern Pacific Bulletin. San Francisco.

Trains. Waukesha, Wis.

Today's Railways. Sheffield, U.K.

Vintage Rails. Waukesha, Wis. [no longer published]

TIMETABLES, BROCHURES, AND ADVERTISEMENTS

Amtrak. Public timetables, 1971 to 2008.

Amtrak. Operating Instructions F40PH/P30CH diesel-electric locomotives, 1983.

Amtrak. Operation Instructions Superliner II, 1993.

Amtrak California. *California Car Operating Manual*, 1997.

Atchison, Topeka & Santa Fe. *Time Schedule No. 6*, 1883.

Atchison, Topeka & Santa Fe. *Coast Lines, Valley Division Employes' [sic] Time Table No. 51*, 1921.

Caltrain. Timetable, 2008.

General Motors. *Electro-Motive Division Model F7 Operating Manual No. 2310*. La Grange, Ill., 1951.

Metrolink. *The Metrolink Story*, 2002.

Metrolink. *Moving Together*, 2004.

Metrolink. *Metrolink Factsheet*, 2008.

Northwestern Pacific. *Timetable 22*, 1943

Pacific Electric Railway. *Employes' [sic] Time Tables . . . "in effect 3.00 A.M., Monday, September 30, 1946 Pacific Standard Time."*

Ride the Train—at the Western Railway Museum, 2005.

Southern Pacific. *Pacific System Time Table No. 17, Coast Division*, 1896.

Southern Pacific. Public timetables, 1930–1958.

Southern Pacific. *Your Daylight Trip*, 1939.

Southern Pacific. *Western Division Timetable 243*, 1947.

Southern Pacific. *Your Daylight Trip, Morning Daylight*, 1949.

Southern Pacific. *Coast Division Timetable 156*, 1949.

Southern Pacific. *Western Region Timetable 3*, 1989.

INTERNET SOURCES

www.ci.pasadena.ca.us

www.eelriver.org/pdf/NCRA_business_plan.pdf

www.gontcd.com

www.lightrail.com

www.nps.gov/history

www.sdmts.com

www.streetcar.org

www.sfmta.com

INDEX